THE
BABA RAMDEV PHENOMENON

Kaushik Deka is a Senior Associate Editor with *India Today*. He hails from Tihu, a sleepy town in lower Assam. An alumnus of the Indian Institute of Mass Communication (IIMC), New Delhi, Deka has earlier co-authored the book *The Secret Killings of Assam*.

THE
BABA RAMDEV
PHENOMENON

FROM MOKSHA
TO MARKET

KAUSHIK DEKA

RUPA

Published by
Rupa Publications India Pvt. Ltd 2017
7/16, Ansari Road, Daryaganj
New Delhi 110002

Sales centres:
Allahabad Bengaluru Chennai
Hyderabad Jaipur Kathmandu
Kolkata Mumbai

ISBN: 978-81-291-4637-3

First impression 2017

10 9 8 7 6 5 4 3 2 1

Printed and bound in India by Repro Knowledgecast Limited, Thane

Contents

Prologue

If I recall correctly, Baba Ramdev first came into my conscience when several members of my extended family in Assam used to talk about the benefits of his yoga module. It was in April 2006. I was in my home state for over a month as I was getting married. There was no work. In fact, I was jobless as nobody except my soon-to-be wife knew that I had quit my job—eighteen days before the wedding—because my employers denied me enough leaves. It offered me an opportunity to interact with my relatives and friends on random issues—being jobless is at times a boon. The marriage arrangements were being taken care of by my father and uncles. Maybe because I was getting married and was going to lose my bachelorhood, or maybe because I was too excited about getting married to someone of my choice, I was diagnosed with high blood pressure.

This is when I heard about Ramdev. Of course, as a journalist I knew about him but I never cared much. My school friend, Tapan Kalita, advised me to do some breathing exercises prescribed by Ramdev. He claimed he had got rid of high blood pressure and lost a few kilos too. A cousin of mine told me that he had the issue of low blood pressure, but the practice of chewing a clove of garlic early in the morning on an empty stomach, as advised by Ramdev, ended his trouble.

I used to ask my father about these, an allopathic doctor, but he never disputed such claims. I found ayurvedic medicines from Ramdev's pharmacy at almost every household I visited around that time. Being the sceptic that I am, I used to ask: 'What religion does this guru preach? What are the rituals you have to follow before taking his medicine? Do you have to feed cows and pigeons?' The answer used to be a resounding 'No'. He never talked religion. It was all about health. I was impressed. For a change, here was a guru who did not sell gods. He sold health. That's actually a nice thing to do.

My next encounter with Ramdev happened in an *India Today* Conclave in 2010. On stage, the then editor of the magazine, Prabhu Chawla, was interviewing him. For the most part, the yoga guru was witty and looked relaxed. He had the audience in splits. As usual, there was the question about his views on homosexuality. I liked the way he answered (of course I did not take any answer seriously)—'*Koi haath tedha karke khana khaaye toh main kya karu.*' (What do I do if someone wants to eat with his hands twisted?) Certainly many were offended, but I never take any comment seriously because I believe in freedom of speech. Problems start when someone tries to enforce his or her views on others.

I saw him once again when he came to the Conclave for the second time in 2012. The very popular author Chetan Bhagat was moderating the session, and this was one occasion where the yoga guru was on the back foot. It was not because he did not have all the answers, but I found Bhagat mercilessly nasty at some points. But the session was one of the best shows of the Conclave. What I liked about Baba was that he did not lose his cool. Most gurus don't like being challenged or mocked at. Ramdev did not care much. In the green room, he was quite cordial with Bhagat. That's the first time I noticed that here was one baba who was ready to make fun of himself. He knew how to take jokes and cracked a few even at himself.

Since then, I had almost forgotten about him until February 2016 when *India Today* Executive Editor S. Sahaya Ranjit asked me to interview Baba Ramdev for our High and Mighty issue. I must confess I was reluctant, but saying no to Ranjit is next to impossible. So I placed a request with Baba's PR team for an interview and waited for them to get back. After some twenty calls to the PR head, one evening, at around 6 p.m., I got a call from Haridwar on my cell phone. Baba was on the line. He greeted me with an 'Om' instead of saying hello, and I, to my surprise, managed to say a 'Namaste'. I'm extremely bad with North Indian greetings and pleasantries, but that day I somehow managed well. The interview began as I introduced my journalistic background and explained to him the intent of the interview. Ramdev was chatty and forthright with his answers. In the middle of the interview, he interrupted my question and asked for my mobile number. I told him that he had called on my number so he should probably have it. But he wanted the number himself, and jotted it down on a paper as I spelt out the number. 'I'm calling you back from my private number,' he said and snapped the call.

Within the next thirty seconds my phone rang again and the interview ran for almost an hour. He laughed uproariously as he explained his mission and, as it happens with me, the discussion veered towards my home state, Assam. He extended me an invitation to visit his ashram. He was also keen to talk about his work in the field of education. I realized he was quite a professional in giving phone interviews as he took pauses long enough for me to take notes without missing anything. He wanted to know his rank in the High and Mighty list, but when I said that I could not reveal it he did not insist.

Three days after this interview, at 6.30 in the morning, his private number flashed on my mobile screen. I thought I was hallucinating. He greeted me with a lot of warmth. I thought he must have called me to find out his rank. But it was my turn to get shocked.

'I want to seek your opinion on an issue,' he said very politely.

'Please ask,' I said though my mind was heavy with anticipation. 'What could it be?'

I cannot reveal what he asked me, as it would be a breach of trust. But as he finished his question, I asked him, 'Why are you asking me this question? You don't know me enough. Why do you think I could give you the correct advice? There are thousands of knowledgeable people in your network.'

His answer was even more astonishing—'We are sanyasi people. We can figure out a person when we speak to him or her. You are an unbiased person. I could sense your santulit (balanced) mind the other day.'

I will be lying if I say I was not flattered. But I was shocked too, because I'm genuinely a person with no opinion in life. I don't believe in forming an opinion without knowing in-depth about a subject, person or event and I know very little of anything. So I'm always the know-nothing person. But why did Baba feel otherwise? The guru must be super smart or I'm exceptionally dumb.

I gave him a detailed answer explaining my logic behind every advice. He sounded happy and in agreement with me. I thought he was trying to sense public mood, as I was a journalist who would have information. Honestly, I could not believe that I was the only person he had consulted for the topic.

A week later, he called me again in the morning to tell me that he took my advice. I did not know how to react. He has not met me ever. *Why is he trusting me so much?* But this behaviour of his also helped me understand him a little better. Despite all his success, business acumen and political connections, he is still childlike in his enthusiasm and probably opens up too easily to strangers. He is still the village boy at heart. He is emotionally charged and gets carried away, often inviting trouble. As time passed, I witnessed more of this later.

Thanks to my High and Mighty list interview, I was assigned the cover story our editorial team had been planning for long on Ramdev. Now I had the opportunity to visit his ashram in Haridwar and my partner in crime was *India Today* Group Photo Editor Bandeep Singh. As usual, I planned to drive overnight to Haridwar and forced Bandeep to accept my travel plan. He was dead against driving at night, but *andhero ko cheerte hue raat ko drive karna* has been my passion. I have often paid a heavy price for this—almost met with a fatal accident, got stuck in riot-hit areas and lost direction.

We left Delhi at midnight and reached Haridwar early in the morning, at around 4.30. It was drizzling. The ashram is an imposing structure spread over 1,000 acres of land. We were taken to the guest house where a nice, spacious room with an AC, TV, fruit basket and complimentary body-care products cost us ₹800 per night. We were asked to rest and told that the Baba would meet us at 7 a.m.

We were at his kutir at 6.50 a.m. The existence of CRPF personnel and physical frisking was in sharp contrast to the serene ambience of his kutir. The only luxury in his humble accommodation was the swing in the verandah. Without wasting a second, I jumped at the swing to relax my body tired from the drive and lack of sleep. But an associate of Ramdev dethroned me saying the swing was only meant for Swamiji. I had my sweet revenge in the evening though.

When I first faced Ramdev for a one-to-one interaction, the yoga guru had just finished an interview with a foreign publication. The reporters had sought the interview with a drone camera. *'Drone laane se kya hoga, sawaal to aakhir homosexuality pe hi poochega. Baaki kaam pe dhyan kam,'* Baba said in what I later realized to be his typical conversational style. And this sets him apart from other gurus. He knows what he is and is comfortable about his position in Indian social and political discourse. He doesn't take himself too seriously and believes in straight talk. There is no copy editor to his statements. That explains a lot of the controversies that he gets involved in.

The next to interview him was popular TV anchor Anuradha Prasad, who is the wife of Congress leader Rajeev Shukla and the sister of BJP Union Minister Ravi Shankar Prasad. As she still needed some footage for her show, and we had to spend the entire day with him, Ramdev decided to take the three of us—Prasad, Bandeep and I—around his ashram to show his educational institutes, gaushalas, organic farms and factories. And he decided to drive himself his Mahindra Scorpio. Bandeep and I were seated in the back seat while Prasad occupied the front passenger seat. 'Swamiji, you are driving and there is a lady next to you. We two are hidden behind. Think of what would happen if TV cameras catch this sight,' I tried to tease the guru. He did not take offence, instead he laughed his heart out.

Suddenly, his phone beeped and it was Acharya Balkrishna on the other end. Ramdev responded in Sanskrit. Perhaps he was trying to hide something from us. Or maybe that's how they love to converse. I asked him if he knew any other language too. 'I'm trying to master English. You need this in international platforms. I also know Nepali and have working knowledge of Marathi, Gujarati and some South Indian languages.' When he talked about his weak English there was no sense of embarrassment. It was simply an acknowledgement of an area he feels he needs to improve in. In modern language, he was 'pretty cool' about being poor in English.

In his gaushala, he showed us the scooter he used to ride when he had started selling his medicines in Haridwar. It was a lucky scooter for him and he would not part with it at any cost. When I asked him to offer me a ride, he happily obliged. I was too curious to know why a sanyasi needed to learn driving or even display his skill sets. 'I'm a sanyasi, not a nikamma (jobless). I will learn everything that helps me do my job better.'

He is certainly not a nikamma and is actually a powerhouse. Bandeep was making Ramdev do a lot of physical activities to get that perfect shot, yet there was no sign of exhaustion or irritation on Baba's face. In his school, Ramdev was asked to play football, badminton, recite shlokas with students and he happily obliged, often giving his own suggestions on getting a better pose and shot. At his organic farm, he tried his hand at ploughing, posed with a nearly 20-kilo pumpkin and played with his cows. Then he treated us to carrots and cucumbers, produced organically at his farm. The taste still remains with me; something I used to feel when I was growing up in my small town in Assam. The breakfast was topped with Patanjali snack bar, which I found a little too sweet but at par with what is already available in the market.

From the farm, he drove us to the big factory where Prasad did her last shoot and left. Once the camerapersons were gone, Baba opened up even more. He waited patiently as Bandeep and his assistant fixed lights, and stood or sat in the same pose, till we got the best shot. In between, he kept responding to the hundreds of questions I threw at him. By late afternoon, we were exhausted, Bandeep was worried because he still had not got his cover shot but Ramdev was brimming with energy. 'Relax, you will get your shot wherever you want. First have lunch,' Ramdev tried to comfort us. He took us to his office where lunch was served. I personally don't enjoy vegetarian food but the home-cooked meal and the freshness of the vegetables made it really delicious.

Post lunch, the three of us—Bandeep, I and another person known to Ramdev—sat in his office for a ten-minute rest. Barring me, the other two were asking him remedies for various ailments. Feeling out of place, I also joined him. 'Swamiji, I want to ask you...'

'Forget it, you will not do anything, it's not in you,' Baba interrupted before I could complete my question. I sat stunned. How did he know this? I have never mentioned that I don't do any exercise. I have never practised yoga in my life, nor do I intend to do so. I never can complete any medicine course because I am forgetful. I have refused free physical training at home. But how could he guess that I would not follow any instructions by him? This is one mystery I have not been able to solve yet and I don't intend to ask him. It's scary to know that someone has figured you out in such detail.

After that brief conversation, we headed back again to his kutir where Bandeep shot that famously viral cover—Ramdev in an upside down position. The idea was to indicate how Ramdev has turned the FMCG market upside down. It was a tough posture to hold for long but Ramdev did it with so much ease. His body is as flexible as rubber. Without any fuss, he gave us all the shots we needed.

After the photo shoot, Balkrishna joined us at Ramdev's kutir. If Ramdev is the bundle of restless energy, Balkrishna is the epitome of calmness. If Ramdev is the public face giving Patanjali the visibility and credibility, Balkrishna is the meticulous planner and executioner of the Patanjali project. In fact, Balkrishna is the sounding board for Brand Ramdev. When I told Balkrishna that Ramdev was driving around a lady, he was visibly annoyed and chided the yoga guru, 'That's how you land up in controversies.'

Balkrishna is the hands-on CEO of Patanjali. He knows his numbers, he travels in luxury—a land rover—uses an iPhone and measures his words. Unlike Ramdev, he doesn't show his emotions. He is also not very comfortable being photographed.

It was now my turn to interview Balkrishna. He sat on the floor and made me sit on the swing from where I had been dethroned in the morning. For a while, Ramdev sat next to me enjoying in silence his closest companion's interview. Then he left for his evening prayers. My eyes, though, were looking for the assistant who had unseated me.

He must know that life and positions can swing any moment.

THE MAKING OF BABA RAMDEV

The Beginning

When in 1965, at Saidalipur, a nondescript village in Haryana, a baby boy was born to a marginal farmer Ram Niwas Yadav and his wife Gulabo Devi, there was hardly any celebration. They were happy to receive what they believed to be the 'most precious gift from God', but there was no time to pause, reflect or celebrate. Life must go on. Little did they realize that the newborn would take this philosophy of detachment to a new height. And if this detachment was induced in their life by poverty and hardship, three decades later their child was to show the world how to practice the same philosophy even when surrounded by unimaginable wealth—nearly ₹10,000 crore.

He was to become Swami Ramdev, one of the most celebrated yoga gurus ever, and also one of India's most influential individuals of this decade. He was to effortlessly straddle between the world of glitter and the world of renunciation, creating a phenomenon the country had never seen before. He was to become the first ever concoction of healthcare, spirituality, business and politics. Forces from these fields have collaborated earlier for common benefits, but never before has there been one individual who embodies the power of all four.

Ramdev's father, a devout Hindu, christened his son Ram Kishen as a mark of his devotion and gratitude to Lord Ram. He prayed regularly, 'Lord Ram, let the blessings of Saraswati always be on him. Please empower my child with education so that he can live a life I could never afford.' The prayers seemed to have a quick effect as Ram Kishen, now learning to spell and count, showed a strong inclination towards words and numbers. He was the brightest student in the government primary school, located in the village, where he studied till the fifth standard. For higher classes he moved to the Shahbajpur High School, a few kilometres away. 'I used to buy second-hand books, yet I always topped my class,' claims Ramdev. Perhaps being at the top is a habit he inculcated too early in life.

Ram Niwas could not have asked for more. The gods were more than pleased with his devotion—his son was rising. But tragedy struck soon. One afternoon, a young Ram Kishen, who had not even celebrated his eighth birthday this was an alien concept for a family which did not keep meticulous birth records—was walking back from school to home with his friends. Suddenly, he felt his left limbs were not where they should be; his left feet did not support his weight, forcing him to fall on the ground cringing with pain. An uncontrollable force pulled his muscles against his wish and even twisted his face. It was as if some ghost entered his body and played havoc with it. It was too late by the time the little boy and his friends could even understand what had hit him. Miles away, when he was taken to a government hospital the next day, the doctors declared—it was a paralytic attack. For the village folks it meant permanent disability…a crippled body, which is good for nothing. A liability for life.

Ram Niwas's world was shattered. He was dreaming of a good education for his son, but now the young boy was not physically fit enough to even be a farmer. 'You were supposed to bring glory to us, the local astrologer had predicted so. So why did Lord Ram punish you? Did we commit any sin?' cried Ram Niwas without realizing that this tragedy was the much-needed catalyst to unfolding a phenomenon the entire country was going to witness thirty years later. That was the first turning point in the journey of Ram Kishen becoming Yoga Guru Ramdev. Today, he drives a Mahindra Scorpio, uses a Micromax mobile and, in his guest houses and anywhere in the ashram, the chosen brands for TVs and ACs are Videocon and Voltas respectively. His modest cottage has four rooms—one to receive guests, one bedroom, one library and a kitchen. The guest room has an AC but it has not been installed in his bedroom. There is a bed, one bookshelf and a study table in his bedroom, but the Baba prefers to sleep on the floor.

❧

First Brush with Yoga

Now that Ram Kishen could not play kabaddi or kushti, unlike his friends, he started spending most of his time in the village library—amid books, mostly on traditional Indian wisdom. One such book was on yoga, which according to the written text claimed that this ancient Indian practice could help one keep control over the mind and body. On one fateful afternoon, Ram Kishen's mind could not command his body to behave—his left side has since refused to take any instruction of his mind—and here was something that could help him regain his hold over his own body. It was a scintillating feeling, as if he had stumbled upon a magic formula.

From the very next day, life changed for Ram Kishen. Like a possessed soul, he began practising the yogic asanas prescribed in the book, a near impossible task for his paralysed body. His rebellious left side did not cooperate at all; the right side writhed in pain and his body bore several bruises, often caused because of loss of balance.

When he was not going through these self-imposed gruelling sessions, he was scouting for new literature on yoga. Books kept piling on and Ram Kishen's obsession with yoga scaled new peaks. And it was not without a reason.

The rebellion from his left side considerably weakened—something the allopathic doctors did not anticipate. He was feeling stronger physically and mentally. Help also came from a local pehalwan in the village akhara, who taught him a few tricks of wrestling. (The training has remained with him throughout his journey, as the young boy grew up to become one of the world's most popular yoga gurus. Whether it's Bollywood star Ranveer Singh in an *Aaj Tak* event or an anchor of a dance show on television, they were at the receiving end of a trademark hand-to-hand combat performance by Ramdev who was once wrestling with paralysis.)

A disobedient body was being disciplined and decorated through a rigorous but determined regime. It was a miracle for the ignorant and the uninitiated as within a decade the young boy reduced his 'permanent disability' to a temporary aberration in his life. He could walk again. Barring the squint in his left eye, Ramdev conquered a paralytic attack. The rebellion of the left was destroyed forever with the power of yoga. That's also one irony in Ramdev's life—before he popularized yoga as an instant thirty-minute drill to cure multiple ailments, he had to wait patiently for over a decade to see results.

But the victory over his left body was not the end of the battle. The boy was now prepared to wage a war against every rebellious body in the world. It was a war against ill health and sick minds. And he had found the Brahmastra—yoga.

But then he was not yet done with the village library. There was another book waiting for him. It was *Satyarth Prakash*, a Hindi book written in 1875 by Maharishi Dayanand Saraswati, the renowned religious and social reformer and the founder of Arya Samaj. If yoga is the physical embodiment of Ramdev, this book formed the intellectual core and social, political and economic philosophy of the yoga guru. It was a book primarily explaining the true tenets of Hinduism, making an appeal for one uniform religion based on the principles of the Vedas. It extolled the greatness of Indian civilization and sought to instill a sense of pride in swadeshi existence. The seed of Ramdev's Patanjali Ayurved's swadeshi motto was first sown in the village library. While greeting someone over phone Ramdev never says hello. Instead he chants 'Om'. The first chapter of Dayanand Saraswati's book explains the etymology and significance of Om.

'This book was a revelation to me. It awakened my inner-self, gave me a sense of purpose in life. It introduced me to the wisdom of our ancestors. I wanted to follow the path shown by the ancient sages,' says Ramdev. The path of ancient sages (rishis) also meant practice of celibacy. So he took a vow—to never marry.

Satyarth Prakash not only changed Ram Kishen's life but also gave it a direction and purpose. He was so moved by the writings of Dayanand Saraswati that he quit the government school where 'the curriculum was a leftover of the education policy' introduced by British politician Thomas

Babington Macaulay (1800–59), who was instrumental in the introduction of English as the medium of instruction for higher education in India.

He knew his parents would never agree to his decision of quitting regular school, where he was doing exceptionally well. So one fine day he fled from home and enrolled himself in a gurukul, a traditional educational institute based on Vedic principles, at Khanpur in Haryana. Under Guru Pradyumna, he learnt Panini's Aadhyayi (the most authentic treatise on Sanskrit grammar), Upanishads, Ayurveda and the Vedas. 'Dayanandji made me realize the value of the treasure trove hidden in Vedic education. It's a progressive approach based on tark (logic), tathya (facts), yukti (argument) and praman (evidence). The goal of British education system was to enslave our mind and curb free and logical thinking,' says Ramdev. 'This is what Gandhiji called swadeshi talim.'

It is here, in this Khanpur gurukul in 1987 that he met for the first time his life-long associate Balkrishna, son of a Brahmin originally hailing from Nepal. It did not take long for the duo to strike friendship—both had intense interest in the Vedas, yoga and Ayurveda. 'He was outgoing but I was reserved. But an eagerness to learn and discover new facts brought us together and we often spent hours debating and discussing life's purpose. We were always intrigued by the power of herbs which eventually took us to Ayurveda,' says Balkrishna. These discussions ended in both wondering: Why am I in this world? What is the purpose of my life?

❧

Awakening in the Himalayas

The answers to Ram Kishen's questions—*Why am I in this world? What is the purpose of my life?*—could not be found in the texts, nor could they come from the gurus. He moved to another gurukul, located in Kalwa in Haryana for further learning. This is where he was given the name Ramdev. 'Guruji (Acharya Baldev) said that my name had both Ram and Krishna. I needed to keep one God in my name. After a lot of thought, I chose Ram because he was the Maryada Purushottam. He was the epitome of sanskar. This is how I became Ramdev,' he says. He may have got a new name but several questions still did not have convincing answers. A young and restless Ram Kishen was desperate to do 'something significant'. Inspired by Dayanand Saraswati, he was seeking a role for himself in the larger scheme of things. When the answer did not come from anywhere, one day, he set out for the Himalayas in search of moksha. 'I was around twenty-five years old then,' says Baba.

He spent three years in the Himalayas, near Gangotri,

meditating, studying herbs and practising yoga. He saw hundreds of other sadhus in the Himalayas, lost in mediation—living a life, which depends on alms for survival.

'I was puzzled. Someone was there for years, lying naked. Someone did not eat for years. But I did not know what they achieved. What was the purpose of gaining knowledge? How were these sadhus contributing to mankind? How did others gain from their knowledge?' said Ramdev, firmly ensconced in the revolving chair in the office of one of his factories.

'The purpose of a sadhu is not to be nikamma and sit idle, rather he has to accomplish bigger tasks for the greater good,' he continues, 'So I came back from the Himalayas because I realized my knowledge will be fruitful only when it's of any use to the people.'

This actually reveals the primary driving force behind Ramdev's empire. Deep inside, he is hurt by a perceptual approach—sadhus can do nothing. They live on others. They are just parasites. He had to show the world what a yogi could do. He had to unleash the power of yoga, the power of spirituality. His journey to the Himalayas was not because he wanted to escape from the world or because he did not have the ability to take care of his social responsibilities. His abilities knew no limits.

'Before going to the Himalayas, my thoughts were concentrated on swayam (self). I wanted nirvana (state of constant happiness) for myself. In the Himalayas, my focus shifted to samashti (group). Collective good became my goal. But the more significant realization was that nirvana is not achieved by just sitting in a jungle.'

He achieved his nirvana. He achieved a higher level of conscience, which taught him that this nirvana was meaningful only when it could result in the welfare of others.

'It was an emotional stage for me. I was experiencing mukti, which is to get rid of desires resulting from ego and ignorance. But this mukti was for me and not for all. I was jeevan-mukt but then why was I living? How can others benefit from my mukti?'

Ramdev found his answer in yoga and spiritualism, what he calls the roots of our ancient civilization. As the roots spread, the journey began and, over the years, several branches came out in the form of Ayurveda, swadeshi movement, organic farming, gau-seva, educational institutes, research and social and political movements. It was time for the yogi to reach out to his people. He was coming to cure them, to enlighten them and to show them the Indian way of living.

'All these originate from the same source—the wisdom of our ancestors, which we had forgotten. This was a natural progression. Whatever I do, it will always have a spiritual connect,' he says.

In 1993, back in Haridwar, a place, in his own words, chosen by destiny, Ramdev began teaching yoga to two men—Yogesh Gupta and V.K. Bansal. One day, their common friend from Surat, Jhivraj Bhai Patel saw the duo practising under Ramdev and was mesmerized. There was a visible change in their appearance; they were leaner, more energetic and their faces, instead of showing stress, as it used to be earlier, were glowing with a sense of peace. Patel requested Ramdev to visit Surat and teach him yoga for a month. Once in Surat, the number of students jumped from just 2 to 200 hundred.

Soon another Gujarati, Rudhrabhai Patel, a diamond merchant, sought him out and this time he helped Ramdev conduct a camp of 2,000 people.

❦

Instant Yoga, Effective Remedies

The number of camps and people attending those camps continued increasing. His yoga was simple—thirty minute morning breathing exercises coupled with a few yoga postures promising faster results, even within a month. He knew what people wanted—continuing good health was not appealing enough, but they were desperate to get rid of common ailments—diabetes, heart issues and obesity. He packaged his offering well—much like instant noodles—and it fitted perfectly with the busy schedule of modern life. What made his success easier was his natural gift of the gab and a sense of humour. He communicated in a language that the mass understood. 'I have always multiplied like this. Such incredible growth has been the hallmark of my journey.' he told me.

In the next couple of years, word of mouth made Ramdev's fame reach till the national capital. In 1995, a mega camp, which was attended by nearly 10,000 people, was organized in Delhi. One Ram Niwas Garg donated ₹5,000 to the yoga guru. This was the first such donation. Till now Ramdev was not charging anything for his yoga tips in the camps, which were organized by his well-wishers. Initially he was reluctant to even accept the donation, but Garg convinced him that it was his small contribution towards fulfilling Ramdev's big dream of obliterating poverty and illiteracy in the country.

'Illiteracy and poverty are the two big ailments hurting the country. There is economic poverty and there is intellectual poverty. Economic poverty is the result of intellectual poverty. Ancient India was a prosperous country because we believed in our wisdom. When we turned our back to our own knowledge, we became a poor nation. We also became illiterate, and not just in terms of education. For instance, there is an illiteracy of nutrition and healthy lifestyle in the country. People eat harmful food, live unhealthy life. As a yogi, it was my duty to take a lead in eradicating poverty and illiteracy from the country.'

As the second step of his mission, Ramdev turned to production of ayurvedic medicine with the ₹5,000 from Garg. He made small packs of Mahasudarshan Churna and headed off to Assam. 'Some of our friends had come back from Assam. They told us how malaria and kalajwar used to kill hundreds there every year. It was a shame in 20th century. So we boarded a train to Assam with the medicine we had made with our own hands. We did not have enough money to use any machine.' Mahasudarshan Churna is known to be extremely effective in the treatment of fever.

In Assam, Ramdev and Balkrishna distributed medicine

in places such as Dibrugarh, Tinsukia and Udalguri. In the 1990s, Bodo insurgent groups had been demanding for a separate Bodoland, and Udalguri was one of their hubs. All outsiders, including the Assamese-speaking people of Assam, were treated with suspicion. There was suspicion among the insurgents that Ramdev and Balkrishna were sent by the Indian government to convince the Bodo population to turn hostile towards the rebels. The duo immediately came under scanner.

'But the bigger troublemakers were the Christian missionary groups. They had a firm grip over the tribal Bodo population living in the remote areas. They panicked because of our presence as they assumed that we had been spreading Hinduism and the tribals will desert them. We had become popular because our medicines were working. Gradually, the insurgent groups understood that we were not government agents and were genuinely benefitting the poor people. By then the missionaries had hatched a plot to kill us. One day, some insurgents came to us and told us that they appreciated our work and would protect us against any conspiracy to harm us,' says Balkrishna.

Years later, many of these insurgents returned to mainstream following a tripartite agreement among the Union government, Assam government and the militants. Bodoland Territorial Autonomous Districts (BTAD) was created by carving out four districts of Assam, and Udalguri was one of them. The rebels formed a political party called Bodoland People's Forum, contested elections and were voted to power to run the Bodoland Territorial

Council, formed for the administration of BTAD, under the 6th Schedule of the Constitution. In 2015, BTC Authority allotted 484.93 hectares of land in Chirang (one of the BTAD districts) to the Patanjali Yogpeeth (Trust). This was for setting up an acharyakulam (school run by the trust), and for the establishment of Cow and Panchagavya Research, for the preservation and promotion of cow breeds and training and collection of medicinal plants. In November 2016, Assam Chief Minister Sarbananda Sonowal laid the foundation stone of the Patanjali Herbal and Mega Food Park at Balipara in Sonitpur district. Patanjali will invest ₹1,300 crore for this facility and promises to provide jobs to 5,000 local people. It is perhaps Ramdev's way of giving back to the state where he first started his Ayurvedic practice.

❧

Ayurveda for the Masses

Later that year in 1997, in Kankhal near Haridwar, Pandit Devi Dutta—his father was a vaidya—and his son Akhilesh gave some bhasma to Ramdev and Balkrishna. The duo started making medicines from this bhasma, but for large-scale manufacturing 15,000 they had neither fund nor infrastructure. So they regularly borrowed money (₹10,000–15,000) from Chatrapati Swami Das of Guru Niwas Ashram. '...because we were sincere and never compromised on the quality of the medicines, these were effective in curing ailments and soon we became popular in Haridwar and nearby areas. We used to make and sell medicines, but our goal was never to make money or profit. Whatever money we earned, we reinvested it or used it to pay our debts.'

But such ad-hoc practices could not continue for long. Ramdev and Balkrishna realized that they needed to get government approval and recognition for manufacturing and selling Ayurvedic medicine. On 10 November 1994, the duo set up 'Yog Sadhna and Chikitsa Shivir' at Swami

Shankardev's Ashram—where they were staying at that time—and started selling medicines. Two months later, on 5 January 1995, they registered Divya Pharmacy, which started with four rooms under a tin shed in Kankhal. Apart from selling medicine, it also functioned as a hospital with four vaidyas. 'The four rooms have become a four-storied building today,' says Ramdev. The initial investment was of ₹5 lakh, of which ₹3.5 lakh came from Ramdev's third disciple, Jhivraj Bhai Patel. Several other disciples donated the remaining amount. 'We continued our sadhna with the feeling of sewa.'

And then came his first experiment with product launch—the innocuous chavanprash, a kind of nutrient and immunity builder for most Indian households. In 1997, Divya Pharmacy started manufacturing chavanprash without any big announcement. There was no advertisement. Those who came to Divya Pharmacy could buy it. It did not have fancy packaging like the other mega brands dominating the market at that time—Dabur and Zandu. There wasn't even an attempt to compete. 'We were not thinking of market or competition. We created it as a preventive medicine. We focused only on quality, finding the right ingredients. It was not business. It is never business for us,' says Balkrishna.

There is an alternative side to the origin of Divya Pharmacy, a version, expectedly not corroborated by Ramdev. *Tehelka* had once published a story elaborating on it. According to it Ramdev, Balkrishna amd Acharya Karamveer had started their journey together sometime in 1990–91 at Tripura Yoga Ashram in Haridwar, where they helped in preparing Ayurvedic medicines. They soon met

Swami Shankar Dev of Kripalu Bagh Ashram, and together they registered a trust called Divya Yog Mandir. They claimed that the Trust aimed to impart practical knowledge of yoga and pranayama. But things started falling apart soon enough. Nine months into the Trust, Balkrishna expelled two of their businessmen on charges of indulging in undesirable activities. Next was Sadhvi Kamla, in 1997, to be shown the door. She was followed by Karamveer, who was forced to resign. Eventually, Ramdev and Balkrishna also convinced Shankar Dev to write that 'in case of division of the trust, the property of the trust will be transferred to a trust with similar intention'. By ousting everybody else, the two became the real owners of the Trust. But there is a footnote to this story—Swami Shankar Dev mysteriously went missing in 2007 and could not be traced.[1]

Whenever I talked to Ramdev about Swami Shankar Dev, I could see pain and desperation in his eyes. According to Ramdev and Balkrishna, Shankar Dev was suffering from several ailments and was in deep pain. He vanished from the ashram one day after his morning walk. 'We filed an FIR immediately. We miss him at every moment in our lives. It was he who gave us a place to stay in Haridwar. He was our guru and in Indian culture, gurus are above everyone,' says Ramdev. Ramdev's other two gurus—Acharya Pradumna and Acharya Baldev, live in two kutirs in Patanjali Yogpeeth—and Ramdev often spends his evenings with the two gurus. On

---

[1]http://www.tehelka.com/2011/06/babas-black-sheep-and-the-golden-fleece/

one summer evening, when I was engrossed in a discussion with Ramdev and Balkrishna in Ramdev's hut, the yoga guru suddenly left. About an hour later, when I looked for him to say bye, I was told that it was his time with his gurus, and so he should be excused.

For the next six years, Ramdev travelled across the country, holding camps, teaching people easy yoga and providing Ayurvedic remedy to almost every ailment. And these were easy remedies—thirty minutes of yoga and a few corrections in the diet chart, coupled with some Ayurvedic medicines wherever needed—and his patients became brand ambassadors for him. 'I was in Patna for some work and when I heard about this camp, I attended it. It was perhaps in 1999. I was suffering from high blood pressure and was on medication. He taught us pranayama and asked me to have garlic on empty stomach in the morning. He did not give me any medicine. Only asked me to stay happy and think positive. I was not sure if I would get results but I tried his method. Within a month, I could see the improvement. It [had] worked,' says Dr Samiran Malla Bujarbaruah from Guwahati in Assam. Bujarbaruah spread the word among all his neighbours and relatives, and they too got desperate to get in touch with him.

Some of his 'patients/followers' from across the nation made trips to his ashram in Haridwar. But for many of them, he was still the Miracle Man they could not reach at will until TV brought him to their living rooms.

❧

India's Celebrity Yoga Guru

It was in 2001. A devotional channel called Sanskar started airing Ramdev's yoga programme at 6.45 in the morning. The 22-minute-long programme soon became the most popular show of the channel. The programme, in fact, created a kind of health revolution in the country. Pranayama became the buzzword for everyone. And the followers were not just fitness enthusiasts or health freaks. From corporate bosses to housewives to students, everyone wanted to practise the yoga packaged by Ramdev—it was easy, short and promised quick results. It stressed on the health benefits of eating vegetables, fruits and herbs regularly. It instilled a sense of pride in the Indian medicinal system. Many liked his prescription. It was not about getting a set of lab tests done by spending huge sums of money. They did not have to buy expensive medicines. Most of the ingredients were easily available and they came cheap. For yoga, they did not have to make big changes in lifestyle. All they needed to do was some exercise and take care of their food quality.

But purists were not amused. Revered yoga guru B.K.S. Iyengar told *India Today* in 2006, 'You cannot have a crash course on yoga. This is not instant coffee. You need years and years of training and religious dedication.'

Soon Ramdev was poached by Astha channel and his popularity kept soaring. In 2002, he held a camp in Delhi with over 10,000 people. By then, his glory had reached the power centres and because of the philosophy he preached, the BJP leadership was naturally drawn towards him. The Delhi camp was attended by the then Delhi Chief Minister Sahib Singh Verma and the then Union HRD Minister Murli Manohar Joshi. In the same camp, he released the monthly magazine *Divya Yoga Sangbad*.

The same year he took Divya Pharmacy to four new places—Delhi, Surat, Ahmedabad and Patna. 'The size of the camps kept increasing. I could see a crowd of over 50,000. Wherever I went, I caused traffic jams. I realized I needed to reach out to people. They saw me on TV but they could not get the medicines through TV. So I decided to set up centres at various places where medicines and primary treatment is easily available. Today, we have 5,000 chikitsalayas and 10,000 sub-centres where medicine and other products are available,' says Ramdev.

From 2004, Astha started telecasting his daily yoga sessions in Haridwar and also the live footage of his camps, and expectedly the public response was massive. From that moment, there was no looking back. The brand of Baba Ramdev was firmly established. Here was a guru who taught yoga, offered Ayurveda cure and came live on TV. He never talked about God or religion; instead he talked about good health. He did not sit on a chair and preach. He did not show instant magic. He did not predict future. Instead, he demonstrated what he preached. He did not advise people to feed pigeons for good fortune, but told them to eat healthy. His medicines were not magical water or secret churna—he came upfront about what he used to make them. 'Before me, yoga gurus like Mahesh Yogi and Rajneesh concentrated on dhyan (meditation) and asanas (yogic postures), which can be difficult to practise. I found pranayama to be the simplest for an average person pressed for time,' said Ramdev in 2006.

What started out as a 22-minute yoga capsule on Sanskar channel culminated with Ramdev setting up his own media empire called Vedic Broadcasting, which runs five TV channels that have become Ramdev's medium for reaching out to a vast audience to extol yoga and ayurveda. He was a baba whom India had never seen before—a hairy, bare-chested man perfecting impossible stunts on stage. He not only smiled but also laughed uproariously. He spoke the common man's language; he was a yogi who was aware of the pains of a family life.

India got its first celebrity yoga guru for the masses.

❧

'Bones' of Contention

Celebration has its share of controversies. And Ramdev's first brush with a big controversy happened in 2004. It was like a precursor to the future. The Baba's right-wing political views were still to come to the fore, but perhaps the perpetual battle between the Left and the Right had already been scripted. CPI(M) leader Brinda Karat accused him of using human and animal bones in some of the Ayurveda medicines produced by Divya Pharmacy.

The controversy started with Karat's support to a group of workers, who were protesting a cut in wages at Ramdev's Divya Pharmacy in Haridwar. It then snowballed into accusations that the ayurvedic medicines prepared at the pharmacy for treating epilepsy and impotence contained powder made from human and animal bones.

Karat sent two samples of the potion to government laboratories to prove her claim. The issue, meanwhile, quickly acquired political overtones with an unusual coalition of political parties and leaders including the BJP, Shiv Sena, the NCP, Mulayam Singh Yadav and Lalu Prasad Yadav taking up cudgels on Ramdev's behalf. 'It really doesn't matter if there are human bones if his medicines can save lives,' averred Lalu. Ramdev did not forget this support. A decade later, he was seen applying his face-glowing cream on Lalu on national television. It could be an act of gratefulness or the yoga guru understood the TRP-grabbing abilities of Lalu Yadav—the self-styled practitioner of buffoonery in Indian politics.

Karat's attack was obfuscated beyond recognition as the massive outpouring of support for Ramdev drowned the charges of labour and medical malpractice levelled by her. Notwithstanding such support, Ramdev's own line of defence was ready and this could unsettle and bewilder even a seasoned communist like Karat. His supporters claimed the CPI(M) and Karat were playing into the hands of MNCs and deliberately attacking him and Ayurveda, as his discourses were adversely impacting the sales of colas. For the first time ever, a communist party and its leader were accused of being hand in glove with American MNCs. And yet, most people seemed to have bought this strange conspiracy theory as Ramdev had by then emerged as the champion of swadeshi movement. In every public platform, he attacked the colas, attributing almost every health disorder to the fizzy drinks. 'Cold drinks have no place in our society; they are basically toilet cleaners. You must get over this western fast food and cold drinks culture,' he said. His logic is that these carbonated colas have a low pH, and because of that these are acidic in nature. These drinks are also carbonated—

added carbon dioxide gas—and, therefore, can cause great harm to one's body system. These acidic drinks are good only for cleaning toilets, a reference to the fact that many people in India use acid to clean toilets.

The controversy fuelled by Karat died a natural death after two different laboratories gave conflicting reports on the presence of bones in the medicines. But Ramdev's battles with colas are not yet over. The all-powerful Rashtriya Swayamsevak Sangh (RSS) and he are putting pressure on the finance and health ministries to impose a heavy tax on beverage companies selling products of high sugar content. They have to their advantage recommendations of the GST panel headed by chief economic adviser to the Union government, Arvind Subramanian, which sought a sin tax of 40 per cent on aerated drinks, tobacco and luxury cars. This rate is more than double of the suggested standard GST rate of 17–18 per cent. Coca-Cola contains 10.6 gm of sugar per 100 ml. That's 26.5 gm (equivalent of five-and-half teaspoons) in a 250 ml can.

In 2016, a study by London-based Action on Sugar (AOS) found the cola giants using double the quantity of sugar in the processed drinks available in India as compared to those in Europe. To cite an example, AOS said Fanta in Ireland, Argentina and the UK had six teaspoons of sugar, whereas the product in India contained almost the double.

The imposition of sin tax is not a new concept, even in India. In July 2016, the Kerala government introduced a 14.5 per cent fat tax on burgers, pizzas, doughnuts and tacos, a move aimed at spreading awareness about obesity and food preferences. Interestingly, levying taxes on high-calorie food items and drinks is one way to rein in consumption.

In 2011, Denmark had introduced a fat tax but repealed it by 2013 when it found consumers were shopping across the border for high-fat goods. Hungary taxes foods high in sugar, salt and fat. Mexico taxes sugary drinks, breakfast cereals and sweets. Taxes on sugary drinks vary across the United States while there is a soda tax in Philadelphia.

❧

Controversies as Catalysts

The Karat controversy, in fact, acted as a catalyst for Ramdev. He emerged as the swadeshi warrior. He became the rallying point of swadeshi pride. Support started pouring in and there was no dearth of funds. In 2006, Ramdev and Balkrishna set up Patanjali Ayurved, which in the next decade was going to rewrite the history of the FMCG sector in India.

The company was named after revered Indian saint Patanjali, who is known to be the author of the *Yoga Sutras*, a text on yoga theory and practice. He belonged to the Samkhya school of Hindu philosophy. He is said to have lived sometime between the 5th century BC and the 4th century BC, with more scholars accepting dates between 2nd and 4th century BC. *Yoga Sutras* has 196 Indian sutras (aphorisms) on yoga. In the medieval era, the book was translated into forty Indian languages. The text fell into obscurity for nearly seven hundred years from the 12th till the 19th century, and made a comeback in late 19th century due to the efforts of Swami Vivekananda and others. Patanjali is also the author of a medical text called *Patanjalatantra*. He is called a medical authority and this text is quoted in many medieval health sciences-related texts.

'We are simply working on the works of Rishi Patanjali by spreading his adhyatyamik (spirituality) with adhunikta (modernity) along with prosperity, science and technology.' Ramdev said in an interview. 'If I wanted name and fame for myself, I could have named the company after me. But we decided to pay tribute to the greatest yogi of all time,' he told me at his ashram.

The first two investments came from one Govind Agarwal (₹1 crore) and one Pappul Pilly (₹7 crore). The initial product lines were medicinal and dairy items. In 2007, the firm took a bank loan of ₹10 crore. The same year, one UK-based couple—Sarwan and Sunita Poddar— offered ₹50 crore to Patanjali for further expansion. In the next three years, Balkrishna's company—he has 94 per cent shareholding while the Poddar family has 6 per cent— received ₹250 crore as investment.

Ramdev recalls how accidents have also played a role in product innovation at Patanjali. In 2006, hundreds of farmers from Mujjafarnagar in Uttar Pradesh met Ramdev. They had lost 500 tons of amla to a thunderstorm. The smart yogi sensed a business opportunity in this disaster. He bought all the amlas, giving relief to the farmers and sent these to Punjab Agro Industries Corporation Limited to produce juice from these amlas. 'Many had suggested [to] me to make pickles, but juice was a better option. There was scepticism if people would accept amla juice, but I knew they would trust my wisdom. I became the brand ambassador of amla juice and the rest is history,' says Ramdev. His yoga camps started promoting amla juice as a remedy to multiple diseases and there was never a dearth of buyers. 'The demand soared the very next year,' says Balkrishna.

In 2009, Patanjali Food and Herbal Park was established under the food park scheme of the Union government. 'Unlike what people say, we did not exactly take advantage of any government policy. We had already started construction of the food park. One day, while I was in a flight, the food-processing minister of the UPA government was seated next to me. I did not even know him. He introduced himself and we started talking. He asked me about my future plans and [I] told him about the food park. He then informed me about the government's policy of encouragement to food parks and I asked my executives to apply for it,' says Ramdev.

One of the largest food parks in the world, it was commissioned at a total investment of ₹500 crore. It is spread across 100 acres and provides employment to over 6,500 people.

According to media reports, the Haridwar plant supplies nearly 60 per cent of the output of Patanjali Ayurved. Every day some 300 trucks roll out of the 150-acre manufacturing complex on the outskirts of Haridwar. The cartons of juices and herbal candy, toothpaste and soap, flour and spices, and a variety of herbal medicines to cure seemingly everything, including headaches, arthritis, asthma and high LDL cholesterol, are destined for sale in every corner of the country. Of course this has added to the transportation cost of these products, but that is likely to go down as Patanjali factories are coming up across the country.

The food park is the nerve centre of Ramdev's business empire where a core team of researchers and managers chalk out the blueprint for next product innovation. For instance, R.S. Shukla, 52, the Hindi-speaking deputy general manager of the business, pulls out a bottle of Power Vite, a competitor to Bournvita or Horlicks, and reels out the names of seven herbs in the product that he claims will strengthen immunity and muscles and stimulate the brain. Armed with a master's degree in chemistry, he looks after the extraction division of the group. Next in line is a small bottle, which has extract of Le Berry, a herb of Ladakh region, which strengthens the cardiac system, prevents cancerous growth and has miraculous injury healing properties. 'We are developing a juice product. It is given as space drink to astronauts in some countries. In India, an aam admi will get it soon,' says Shukla.

Then there is Hemanta Kumar, a thirty-five-year-old PhD holder in biochemistry, who heads the herbal research and genomics division. Venkatesh Shankar, 45, a physicist from Bhabha Atomic Research Centre, who has worked for fifteen years in Hindustan Unilever and is now the head of Patanjali's home and personal care divisions including research. He plans to take the turnover of his division from 1,000 to 1,700 crores in 2017 by adding forty more products to the existing list of eighty. Muniraj Singh Pundir, 41, an M.Tech who worked abroad, heads the biscuits and confectionary division. 'There are various production units and R&D

facilities where we've employed 200 scientists. People say Babaji still sleeps on the floor but he has employed scientists at salaries of 50 lakh to a crore per year,' Ramdev told *The Indian Express.*

❧

FROM MOKSHA TO MARKET

Patanjali: The New FMCG King

With nearly 10 lakh active followers across India, Ramdev's foray into the FMCG sector through Patanjali Ayurved has caused an upheaval among the established players such as Hindustan Unilever Limited (HUL), Nestlé and Dabur. The last time a new entrant created such noise was ITC's entry into the consumer segment in the late 1990s. Long before that, in the 1980s, detergent brand Nirma challenged HUL products in the same category. But Ramdev's retail launch with more than 400 products—including shampoo, toothpaste, ghee, detergent, biscuit, cereals and anti-ageing creams—under its belt, seeks to even rewrite the norms of FMCG market. Patanjali claims that all the products manufactured by it are made from Ayurveda and natural components. According to multinational brokerage company CLSA, Patanjali is the fastest growing fast-moving consumer goods company in India. It is valued at ₹13,000 crore.

Revenue of Patanjali Over the Years

Year	Turnover
2009–10	₹163 crore
2010–11	₹317 crore
2011–12	₹450 crore
2012–13	₹ 849 crore
2013–14	₹1,191 crore
2014–15	₹2,006 crore
2015–16	₹5,000 crore

From a turnover of ₹450 crore in 2012, Patanjali Ayurved has clocked ₹5,000 crore in March 2016, showing an eleven-fold growth. Of course Patanjali is yet to break into the league of big players such as Hindustan Unilever (₹31,000 crore), Godrej Consumer Products (₹9,000 crore), Dabur India (₹8,450 crore), Nestlé India (₹8,200 crore) and Marico Industries (₹6,100 crore). But if the records of past few years are analysed, it may not take long for it to reach as far. Sales climbed up steadily from a humble ₹453 crore in 2011–12 to ₹849 crore in 2012–13, to ₹1,191 crore in 2013–14, to ₹2,006 crore 2014–15, and finally to the astounding ₹5,000 crore mark. No other FMCG company has been able to achieve such organic growth in recent times.

Global MNCs have begun to take note of Patanjali's impact. Umesh Phadke, CEO of the Indonesian unit of L'Oréal, said he had his eyes opened when he visited the first Patanjali Ayurved megastore in India in 2016. 'The long-term sustainability of the whole enterprise is open to debate. In the short term, this brand will significantly impact all of us multinationals,' he wrote on his personal Facebook page in October 2016.

'Any large MNC operating in this space generally looks at a gross margin (profit before tax)—after corporate overheads of 10 per cent and marketing/advertising expenditure of approximately 13 per cent—of approximately 20 per cent. As against this, Patanjali is thought by industry analysts to be operating at less than 10 per cent margin, (corporate overheads are said to be low and Ramdev and Balkrishna take no salary) and less than 5 per cent marketing spends. The net savings thus amount to 25 per cent. Not surprising then that the brand is able to offer products like honey, shampoos and toothpastes at a 25 per cent discount to the market leader,' says Ambi Parameswaran, brand strategist and founder of brand-building.com.

'We could reduce our cost for four reasons. We don't have high-flying executives who spend 90 per cent of their time in conference calls and making presentations. Our purchase department has men of integrity. Till now we kept our distribution network restricted to our flagship stores,' explains Ramdev. According to Acharya Balkrishna, the managing director of Patanjali Ayurved, profits will be reinvested in innovation and capacity expansion so that prices can be brought down further. The company now operates at an 8–10 per cent profit margin.

According to a report by Nielsen—'Anticipate with Analytics: The Future of FMCG'[2]—growth margins for the big brands in this sector have diminished, leading to growth at a pace far slower than FMCG companies are used to. India's entire packaged consumer products market is estimated at about ₹3.2 lakh crore a year, according to a September 2015 report by Federation of Indian Chambers of Commerce and Industry and advisory firm KPMG. All major players have been hit; HUL's revenue growth in the past seven quarters has consistently fallen, from 13.2 per cent in June 2014 to 3.2 per cent now. ITC's non-cigarette FMCG business has fallen from 11–12 per cent then to 7 per cent now.

Contrast this with Patanjali. In the last one year, its sales have more than doubled while its biggest competitor HUL's sales rose by 4 per cent. ITC's FMCG segment, other than cigarettes, grew at 7.7 per cent between 2014 and 2015.

The incredible success of brand Patanjali results from the credibility Ramdev has earned as a yoga guru and Ayurvedic practitioner among millions of his followers. It's also benefitting from an emerging health consciousness, which has resulted in a shift in consumer preferences towards herbal and ayurvedic products. Added to that is the swadeshi slogan—Ramdev markets his products as an assault on the

---

[2]http://www.nielsen.com/in/en/insights/reports/2015/anticipate-with-analytics-the-future-of-fmcg.html

foreign MNCs, which are here to 'loot Indian customers'. He appeals to the Indian pride when he says, 'I will make the MNCs do shirshasana.'

'Our internal economy is under control of these foreign companies—whether it is Monsanto in agriculture or in automobiles, mobile, technical, IT, health, medicines, machinery and equipment, they have not spared any field. We [India] import about ₹25 lakh crore worth of goods. That is, foreign companies have captured ₹25 lakh crore of our internal economy. Our dream is to bring economic independence to our country. We want to save our country from political slavery and work with this commitment,' says Ramdev.

And Ramdev is not done yet as he expects to double the turnover next year. Patanjali Ayurved's goal is to scale up its production to ₹1 lakh crore by 2020. According to Ramdev, it's not an impossible feat as Patanjali has been registering 100 per cent growth for the last four years. The current objective is reported to be 50,000 crore in the next two to three years for in-house production.

According to Balkrishna, Patanjali aims to clock sales of 40,000 crore by the financial year 2018–19. That growth target translates into a doubling of the turnover every year, for the next three years. An IIFL Institutional Equities report estimates that Patanjali's sales will increase to 20,000 crore by 2020. It will garner double-digit market share in 10 of the 25 categories. Patanjali has already garnered more than 5 per cent market share, which will further increase to 13 per cent by 2020.

A report by Edelweiss, a financial services provider, states: 'The company is working on plugging the gaps in the supply chain and distribution with plans afoot to implement ERP (for better inventory management) and consolidate its online presence. Strong innovation and new products pipeline, pricing discounts to the peers (15%–30%) ayurvedic and natural propositions with low A&P spends (leveraging Baba Ramdev's brand pull) lend Patanjali's products an edge over competition. However, distribution remains a key monitorable.'

A report by HSBC Securities and Capital Markets (India) states: 'The company's business model is rewriting the rules of consumer marketing in India. We think rapid growth will continue, driven by an ever-increasing consumer demand for its products; the launch of new categories; and a broader retail and distribution network (two-thirds of revenue comes from northern India).'

The impact is visible in the reports of rival companies. Toothpaste maker Colgate, which has around 57 per cent market share, saw a dip in its sales growth from double digit between 2005 and 2015 to just 3.7 per cent in the first nine months of FY16, as Patanjali's Dant Kanti made inroads. Its FY15 sales growth was 11.8 per cent, lowest in a decade. Even Swadeshi Jagran Manch co-founder, S. Gurumurthy who says: 'He has changed the rules of the game forcing even the MNC's to follow him. The Colgate ad now talks about neem and salt in toothpaste.'

According to a recent report by *India Infoline*, Patanjali will hit at least thirteen listed companies. IIFL says that 11 per cent of Patanjali's FY20 turnover will come at the cost of HUL alone.

Not surprisingly, an ASSOCHAM-TechSci Research Paper has declared Patanjali Ayurved as the the most disruptive force in India's fast moving consumer goods market, which is expected to reach the US$ billion mark by 2020. It has expanded its product portfolio across wide range of personal care and food and beverages witnessed a whopping annual growth of 146 per cent in FY2016 grossing in turnover of US$ 769 million whereas its peers including ITC, Dabur, Hindustan Unilever, Colgate-Palmolive and Procter & Gamble, among others, struggled to get a growth much less than a double digit.

'Patanjali Ayurved has turned out to be the most disruptive force in the Indian FMCG market. Initially the company focused only on the development of Ayurvedic medicines but gradually started manufacturing food items and cosmetics,' says the report. 'Many of its product launches have impacted the shares of other FMCG companies in that product category. Some of its flagship brands which have wrested the market share of its competitors include Dant Kranti, Atta noodles and Kesh Kranti,' the paper said.

'Like in several other areas, the Indian FMCG is also witnessing its disruptive moments. Interestingly, the big disruption has come about from unconventional ownership. Yet another interesting aspect is that unlike a few years ago, the focus has shifted away from the foreign direct investment in multi-brand retail to home-grown Ayurveda. This also reflects a kind of latent desire among the Indian consumers to adopt the products which are safe, healthy and free from side-effects,' said ASSOCHAM Secretary General D.S. Rawat in a newspaper report.

According to the ASSOCHAM report, the total Indian FMCG market in 2015 was US\$ 43 billion of which 60 per cent was concentrated in urban areas and the rest in the rural areas. And it seems Patanjali has been able to capture the imagination of rural India. According to the Rural Establishment Survey conducted by Chrome Data Analytics that claims to cover over 200,000 villages with over 300 million consumers, 93 per cent rural households are aware of Patanjali but more than half, 56 per cent, do not know about at least 30 per cent of its products.

The Organizational Spread of Patanjali

- Patanjali Yogpeeth, Haridwar (with centres in Ranchi, Kolkata, Guwahati, UK, USA, Canada, Nepal and Mauritius)
- Divya Pharmacy
- Patanjali Ayurved College and Hospital
- University of Patanjali
- Acharya Kulam
- Patanjali Research Institute
- Patanjali Herbal Garden & Research Center
- Patanjali Research Foundation
- Gaushala Agriculture Farm
- Patanjali Gramudyog Trust
- Bharat Swabhiman Trust

- Patanjali Sevashram, Mulya, Devprayag
- Yog Gram, Sidcul, Haridwar
- Meditation Center, Gangotri
- Gurukul Ghasera, Rewari, Haryana
- Patanjali Chikitsalay (dispensaries), Patanjali Aryogya-kendra (pharmacy) and Patanjali Mega Store (across the country)
- Vedic Education Research Institute
- Vedic Broadcasting Ltd

Source: Author

Table 2: The Business Empire of Baba Ramdev

	Company Name	Date of Incorporation	Annual Turnover (₹crore)	What It Manufactures	Ownership Details
1	Patanjali Ayurved Limited	13/01/2006	5,000	Wide range of products from ayurvedic medicines to shampoos and detergents to cereals	Acharya Balkrishna, Mukta Nand, Ajai Kumar Arya, Rakesh Mittal, Sumedha, Yaj Dev Arya, Shashi Chandra Jha
2	Patanjali Biscuit	09/01/2009	Subsidiary of Patanjali Ayurved, turnover included in Patanjali Ayurved	Biscuits	Suresh Kailashchand Agarwal, Ashok Kumar Agarwal, Ajay Kumar Ghosh, Ram Bharat, Yash Dev Arya

3	Patanjali Arogya Private Limited	19/08/2009	NA	Not functional yet	Ram Bharat, Acharya Balkrishna
4	Patanjali Agro Arya Limited	19/08/2009	NA	Not functional yet	Ram Bharat, Rajendra Kumar Agrawal, Aacharya Ganeshji
5	Patanjali Aromatics Private Limited	20/08/2009	NA	Not functional yet	Ram Bharat, Acharya Balkrishna
6	Patanjali Madhuram Udyog Private Limited	21/03/2011	NA	Not functional yet	Ram Bharat, Acharya Balkrishna
7	Patanjali Paridhan Private Limited	21/08/2009	NA	Not functional yet	Ram Bharat, Acharya Balkrishna
8	Patanjali Parivahan Private Limited	21/08/2009	8-10	Transportation	Ram Bharat, Siddhartha Ananta Bhargava, Yash Dev Arya

	Company Name	Date of Incorporation	Annual Turnover (`crore)	What It Manufactures	Ownership Details
9	Patanjali Peya Private Limited	24/08/2009	NA	Not functional	Ram Bharat, Acharya Balkrishna
10	Patanjali Textiles Private Limited	24/08/2009		Not functional	Ram Bharat, Acharya Balkrishna
11	Patanjali Food and Herbal Park Limited	27/01/2009	NA	Herbal food products	Sudhir Kumar Aggarwal, Sunil Kumar Chaturvedi, Devendra Kumar, Acharya Balkrishna, Mukta Nand, Bhupesh Chandra Tewari, Raj Kumar Pandey
12	Patanjali Bio Research Institute Private Limited	11/03/2011	18–20	Organic products	Gowdara Paran Gowda, Aacharya Ganeshji, Akhilesh Shivpuri

| 13 | Patanjali Agroherbal Research Private Limited | 20/04/2009 | NA | Herbal plantations, no commercial activity yet | Lokesh Sharma, Moti Sharma |
| 14 | Patanjali Natural Coloroma Private Limited | 17/12/2009 | 7–8 | Natural colour extracts | Indermohan Aggarwal, Siddhartha Ananta Bhargava, Rakesh Mittal |

Source: Author

The Success Mantra

Patanjali's strategy relies on spreading itself thin aross dozens of FMCG categories and carpet-bombing consumers with scores of products, rather than on focussing its energies on one or two large wins. 'There are three important factors behind the success of Patanjali. We never compromise on these three. Firstly, we have world-class infrastructure, research labs and scientists. We follow strict procedures to do world-class research, build a world-class setup and maintain world-class quality parameters. Secondly, our raw material procurement is one of the most crucial functions. A lot of disorders and malfunctions can happen in this stage and it could affect the quality of the product. We have a trusted and reliable team of people with 20–25 years experience of procurement. The people involved in raw material purchase are of unquestionable integrity. They take care that quality in raw material is never compromised. Thirdly, whatever we earn and whatever is our profit, we utilize 100 per cent of it in the service of people. I am an unpaid brand ambassador and Acharya Balkrishna is the managing director and a shareholder. No salary, no dividend. This is the first time it is happening in any business organization as normally any business house or corporate house has a motive to earn more profits and increase prosperity,' explains Ramdev. Still, as per *Forbes* magazine, Balkrishna's net worth is $2.5 billion (I've written more about him in the next section).

Meanwhile, Patanjali's portfolio spans personal care products, toothpastes, home cleaning products, dishwash and detergents, staples such as atta, salt, cooking oil and tea, juices and dairy products, apart from a range of ayurvedic formulations.

'The Patanjali brand straddles numerous categories and has therefore created a larger-than-life image for the brand. And it is possible that these multiple offerings help each other,' mentions a report. It is believed that most of the ₹5,000 crore sales comes from just three products—ghee, toothpaste and hair oil/shampoo. But offering a multitude of products has helped build a strong brand aura.

Patanjali Revenue Break-Up	
Food	37%
Healthcare	19%
Toiletries	15%
Dental products	11%
Hair care	11%
Cosmetics	7%

'There is a different dynamic here that must also be considered—because of Baba Ramdev's telegenic personality that cuts through the socio-cultural and economic layers of our complex country, we are probably seeing diverse classes of consumers adopting a brand for the first time in their lives. The immense popularity of Patanjali ghee points to the fact that Baba Ramdev has managed to convert millions of consumers from unorganized, unbranded, loose (sold in loose form) product purchase to a branded packaged purchase. This is a tremendous movement. It is also possible that poor consumers who were not comfortable with buying a 'videshi' shampoo or toothpaste, are willing and happy to purchase a Patanjali shampoo and toothpaste. The same may now apply to jeans. In marketing text books, this is called 'brandification' of a category. When Hindustan Lever launched Rin detergent bars, they managed to convert consumers from unbranded soap bars to a branded detergent bar. Today, large FMCG players are perhaps not innovative enough with new products, new variants, new offers—they tend to play it safe. Baba Ramdev has filled that gap,' writes Ambi Parameswaran of brand-building.com.

Patanjali's initial success has been the result of the fact that it has been able to tackle some of these traditional issues. It has consistently advertised its products harping on quality and purity, thereby hoping to dispel consumers' doubts on that score. And it has managed to keep prices low. Most importantly, it has consistently communicated the special features of its products as well as the price. It is currently aggressively advertising its honey as 43 per cent cheaper than

Dabur honey for a 250 ml pack. For the 500 ml category, the price difference is 32 per cent.

Until 2015, Patanjali's business model was very distinct from the MNCs that it loves to loathe. Patanjali products are sold through three types of centres—Patanjali Chikitsalaya, which are clinics with doctors, Patanjali Arogya Kendra, which are health and wellness centres, and Swadeshi Kendra, non-medicine outlets. A typical Patanjali centre is 500 to 1,500 square feet in size. The group has 15,000 exclusive outlets across India. They plan to grow to 100,000 outlets in the next few years. A Credit Lyonnais Securities Asia (CLSA) report quoted retailers claiming that their average gross turnover was ₹25,000 everyday. Profit margins for retailers are 10–20 per cent across product categories.

Patanjali's umbrella branding strategy has helped it gain loyal consumers among Ramdev's followers and those who believe in buying swadeshi products. But Ramdev understands that if Patanjali has to succeed in its ambitious plans of giving the MNCs a run for their money, it cannot solely depend on its quaint practices. A national presence requires substantial investment in manufacturing units in southern, western and eastern India. Word-of-mouth may need to be supplemented with a national advertising campaign.

Distribution also plays a huge role in the sucess of Patanjali products. In April 2016, Mumbai-based Pittie Group, the nationwide distributor for Patanjali products, sewed up a distribution arrangement with Apollo Pharmacy. It also has a marketing arrangement with Kishore Biyani's Future Retail Ltd for selling Patanjali products in 243 cities across India. It took a phone call from Ramdev in the summer of 2015 and two successive visits to the Patanjali factory in Haridwar to convice Biyani to sell Patanjali products. Future Group sells about ₹30 crore worth of the company's products every month. Patanjali Ayurved has also teamed up with billionaire Mukesh Ambani's retail chain Reliance Retail to sell its products. In an interaction with the *Times of India*, Damodar Mall, CEO of Reliance Retail, admits that while they were sceptical about Patanjali products for supermarket customers, they have been surprised by 'the level of traction' his products have received at the stores.

☙

Acharya Balkrishna: The Brain Behind Patanjali's Rise

If Ramdev has been the face of Patanjali, Balkrishna has been the meticulous planner and anchor whenever there has been a drift, even by the yoga guru himself. If Ramdev has been the camera friendly, vocal campaigner of Patanjali, Balakrishna believes in staying behind the scenes and measuring every word Ramdev utters. Always dressed in a white tunic and dhoti, the MD of Patanjali has his eyes fixed on every detail; nothing escapes his scrutiny. 'What was the need to do such antics? TV cameras could have given it a twisted angle,' Balkrishna had chided Ramdev when he learnt that earlier in that day the yoga guru had driven around a woman journalist in his SUV. Interestigly, the journalist is the wife of a senior leader of Congress, a party Ramdev has little love lost.

Born as Balkrishna Suvedi, to Sumitra Devi and Jay Vallabh—Nepali citizens who later shifted to India—he is the managing director of 34 companies under the Patanjali group. He is also the vice-chancellor of Patanjali University and heads various other trusts and institutes. Balkrishna's office is in a corridor of the 200-bed Ayurveda hospital, a short drive from the manufacturing factory. Across the street is a 10-acre nursery he oversees, where nearly a thousand varieties of plants are grown and studied. He is also developing a new research lab to study the medicinal properties of several yet-to-be explored herbs.

His father was working as a security guard at an ashram in Haridwar when Balkrishna was born, one of six brothers. They moved back to their village in Nepal soon after and are settled there as farmers. 'By birth, I'm an Indian,' says Balkrishna who returned to India at the age of twelve, when he first met Ramdev in their gurukul. Like Ramdev, after his stint in the gurukul, Balkrishna went to the Himalayas, not seeking moksha but to study plants and to experiment with their medicinal value. Ayurveda was the call of his life. Among other achievements, Patanjali interestingly claims that Balkrishna rediscovered the Sanjivani booti[3]—the famed herb that saved the life of the mythological character Lakshman.

'When we were students we never thought we wanted to become very big businessmen or make a lot of money; that was never our mindset. We didn't come from any major family background. Had that been our thought, we

---

[3]http://www.hindustantimes.com/india/has-ramdev-done-what-hanuman-couldn-t/story-yqCE0scK7Lvc7xxTkgdhQI.html

would never have gone to a gurukul. Everyone knows by going to a gurukul and studying Sanskrit, no one becomes rich. We went to a gurukul thinking we'll become experts in our ancient texts and philosophies,' Balkrishna said in an interview with the *Forbes* magazine. According to the magazine, Balkrishna, who owns 98.5 per cent of the unlisted company, is the 48th richest person in the country, with an estimated wealth of $2.5 billion or ₹25,600 crore.[4] 'We want to use this wealth to serve others and not ourselves. But at the same time we don't believe in giving things for free because, if we did that, within a year we'd be back to going around with a begging bowl. We need the wealth to serve the people,' he told *Forbes*.

Together with Ramdev, he monitors the innovation and evolution of every product and even approves the final design for packaging. Ramdev even turns copywriter for several product-selling booklets.

THE OTHER IMPORTANT PLAYERS

The third pillar in this success story has been Ram Bharat, 39, Ramdev's reclusive younger brother who avoids being photographed and refuses interview requests. Ram Bharat first came into the limelight in May 2016 when he was sent to judicial custody on charges of instigating a clash between a Haridwar truck union and guards at the factory, which ended in one person's death and four injured people.

He looks after the day-to-day management of two units

---

[4]http://www.forbes.com/profile/acharya-balkrishna/

of Patanjali Yogpeeth in Haridwar from a huge wood-crafted office. Started in 2006 and spread over an area of 1,000 acres, it now houses Patanjali Ayurved factory and research centre, a ghee-producing unit, a university, a school, two gurukuls, a gaushala, a Bharat Mata Naman Sthal and a food park, which has nine giant units of food, consumer home and cosmetic products and a testing laboratory. Nearly 15,000 people, including top-level managers, are employed there.

If Ramdev is making a claim of ₹10,000 crore turnover by next year, he has the backing of the meticulous planning of Balaram Singh Kushwaha, business head of the sales and marketing division of Patanjali Ayurved, who was earlier with Hindustan Unilever and Gillette. 'The in-house supply outlets would double to 10,000 by next year and the private store coverage would jump from ₹1.60 lakh to ₹8 lakh and distributor network from 2,000 to 4,300. We would also have our own warehouses in all the major state capitals,' he says.

Several insiders claim that the success of Patanjali in the field of Ayurveda must be attributed to Swami Muktanand, one of the directors of Patanjali. Born in West Bengal, he looks after the production of medicines in Patanjali. He specializes in the preparation of chavanprash and amrit rasayan. Swami Muktanand is on the board of ten companies as a director.

Inside the Yogpeeth, 350 research scholars including 100 with PhD degrees have been working in various fields like herbal medicine, yoga, ancient manuscripts, natural cosmetics, food, home care, and naturopathy, drawing a monthly salary between ₹30,000 to ₹3.5 lakh.

On 9 February 2017, Patanjali Yogpeeth, registered as a public charitable trust, won an appeal before the Income Tax Appellate Tribunal (ITAT), which exempted it from paying income tax. The ITAT (Delhi bench) held that yoga entails providing medical relief and camps also provide education, and that both 'medical relief' and 'imparting education' fall within the meaning of charitable purpose, entitling the trust to claim I-T exempt status under sections 11 and 12 of the Income Tax Act. What came to Patanjali's favour was the amendment in the I-T Act, which came into effect from 1 April 2016. This amendment specifically inserted yoga within the definition of 'charitable purpose'.

The ITAT also held that corpus donations aggregating to ₹43.98 crore received by Patanjali Yogpeeth, predominantly for construction of cottages under its Vanprasth Ashram Scheme (which provides accommodation to those attending residential yoga courses), were capital receipts not liable to I-T. Such donations included land donated, whose market value was pegged by I-T authorities at ₹65 lakh. The ITAT also agreed with the submissions made by the trust and observed that certain inferences by the I-T authorities such as provision of benefits to certain persons or receipt of anonymous donations were made without fully appreciating the facts. Various additions to the trust's income made by the I-T authorities, including a ₹96 lakh addition made for services made by the trust to Vedic Broadcasting in which Acharya Balkrishnan, a trustee and close aide of Baba

Ramdev, holds substantial interest were deleted by the ITAT, on the ground that the I-T authorities had not understood the facts.

❦

Challenging the Challenger

The MNCs are gearing up to the challenge thrown by Patanjali. Hindustan Unilever, India's largest consumer goods company, is launching a raft of Ayurvedic personal care products aimed at the product portfolio of Patanjali. It will launch around twenty products—toothpaste and skin cream to soaps and shampoos—under its existing Ayurveda brand Ayush. Ayush was launched in 2001 as a premium brand but had lost momentum by 2007. Now, the positioning will be mass market—price points between ₹30 and ₹130. These twenty products are being launched in stores across the South Indian states of Karnataka, Kerala, Tamil Nadu, Andhra Pradesh, and Telangana.

'The new range of Lever Ayush brings 5,000 years of Ayurvedic wisdom to solve modern lifestyle problems. The products are designed to attract and retain such consumers with high-quality Ayurveda-based offerings,' a company release mentioned. The company also acquired ayurvedic hair oil brand Indulekha from Mosons Group in 2016[5], which it is rapidly expanding across markets.

Unilever's hold on India's $11.7 billion beauty and personal care market has slipped more than 5 percentage points in the past five years, according to researcher Euromonitor International. And local personal care rival Dabur India Ltd says its growth is slowing, even as the market is believed to have expanded 14 per cent in 2016. Patanjali had a 1.2 per cent share of India's beauty and personal care market in 2015 from 0.2 per cent in 2011, according to Euromonitor.

This is not the first time Hindustan Unilever has taken on a desi challenger. In the mid-1980s, Ahmedabad-based Karsanbhai Patel's Nirma, a detergent brand, toppled HUL's Surf from the shelves of middle class and lower middle class Indian homes. The Indian unit of the Anglo-Dutch FMCG company then rolled out Wheel, a low-priced option. The battle between Nirma and Wheel is a part of corporate and advertising folklore.

HUL's personal care business accounts for nearly half of its sales and 60 per cent profits, mainly due to a large portfolio of premium products. Herbal products account for 6–7 per cent of HUL's personal products segment. The Indian herbal products market that is estimated to be around $6.4 billion in 2016, may grow to $7.6 billion by 2020,

---

[5]http://timesofindia.indiatimes.com/business/india-business/ HUL-acquired-Indulekha-Vayodha-from-Mosons-Group/ articleshow/50219359.cms

according to a FICCI-PWC study. The segment is growing at almost twice the rate of the overall FMCG market.

Patanjali's rise has led to others exploring the Ayurveda and herbal products space. L'Oréal launched a hair care range under Garnier Ultra Blends made with 'natural ingredients'. Godrej Consumer Products plans to launch herbal variants across product categories. It has already launched neem-based household insecticides and a toilet soap variant with neem and coconut oil.

It seems that Colgate-Palmolive India is feeling the heat of the 'natural' revolution ushered in by Patanjali Ayurved. The personal and oral care giant has launched a new all-herbal and indigenous toothpaste under the Cibaca brand, arguably to fend off competition by Patanjali Dant Kanti. With clove, basil, lemon, camphor, eucalyptus and thymol, the product not only has a formulation that is very Indian, but also quite an Indian name—Colgate Cibaca Vedshakti.

Colgate also came up with an advertisement for Vedshakti which has a tagline—'*Kudrat Ka Saath, Swastha Aur Surakshit Daant*'. While Colgate has been selling herbal variants such as neem and clove in the country, this is the first indigenous brand in the ayurvedic segment for the US $16 billion global giant that controls more than half the oral care market in India. Colgate has global experience in natural segment, having acquired Tom's of Maine in the US a decade ago, while Colgate Mishvak is present in Turkey, Indonesia and elsewhere. It also has a wider reach. Patanjali has products in 2 lakh traditional retail outlets while Colgate has access to more than 50 lakh stores.

Ramdev is not amused with the challenge and competition. In anticipation of the launch of Colgate's new all-herbal and indigenous toothpaste, he reacted on Twitter: 'Colgate used to warn against Indian traditional ways of using salt and coal on teeth. But now, it actively endorses it.' Substantiating his tweet was a collage of an old Colgate toothpaste ad (1985) carrying the above 'warning' against salt and coal, as well as new ones in which model and actor Lara Dutta can be seen endorsing Colgate's Active Salt and Colgate Total Charcoal Deep Clean toothpastes.

Certainly, Patanjali's sales growth rates in the last three years have been soaring, with revenues growing at a 55 per cent annual rate when the FMCG market was inching up at 8–9 per cent. But these growth rates have to be seen in the context of a low base, and the vast product portfolio that Patanjali relies on for its critical mass.

Though Patanjali's current size has created this perception that it has already captured big market share at the cost of the MNCs, this is only partially true. In the food or dairy categories, where Patanjali has made significant inroads, there is little MNC presence. *India Infoline* has said that the company could grab 35 per cent of both the Indian honey and ayurvedic medicine markets, and a third of the market for ghee, a type of clarified butter. Also, that Colgate-Palmolive and Dabur would be hurt the most by Patanjali's expansion.

According to a 2017 survey by Edelweiss Securities, natural positioning and attractive pricing have helped Patanjali wrest market share from players such as Dabur,

Colgate and HUL. According to the survey, 83 per cent users prefer Patanjali products due to their natural positioning, while 38 per cent because of attractive pricing. As many as 91 per cent respondents find natural products better and 67 per cent are ready to pay a premium for them, indicating that natural, and especially affordable naturals, should remain the key focus area for consumer goods companies to prevent market share loss and achieve better growth.

The Herbal Hustle: Toothpaste Category

According to a report by ICICI Securities, Patanjali's entry has disrupted the toothpaste category in India, denting Colgate's market share by approximately 150 basis points from 57.2 per cent in 2015 to 55.7 per cent in March 2016. However, a second report by Edelweiss Securities points out that other herbal player, Dabur, could also have contributed to the decline. When Colgate's volume growth had slowed down to a low single digit, Dabur's oral care portfolio was clocking double digit growth, it stated.

The above findings are also corroborated by Nielsen's analysis across five prominent personal care categories, which indicate that the natural segment now constitutes about a third of total sales, and is growing at 2.5 times of non-naturals in India. As per the report by ICICI Securities, the rural population accounts for approximately 35 per cent toothpaste revenue for

Colgate-Palmolive India. However, there is still huge opportunity for brands in rural markets where overall toothpaste penetration stood at just 74.1 per cent in 2014, as opposed to 92.3 per cent the same year in urban India. Patanjali's rural reach, as mentioned earlier, gives it an edge over others.

Further, various reports peg Patanjali's market share at 4.5–5 per cent and Colgate's share in the natural segment, where it is present with Colgate Active Salt, Active Salt Neem, and Active Salt Healthy White Toothpaste, at 7 per cent. The competition is pretty close.

Patanjali's Dantkanti claims to have generated business worth ₹450 crore in 2015–16. Currently, four variants, namely, Danti Kanti Regular (13 herbs), Dant Kanti Advanced (26 herbs), Patanjali Medicated Gel, and Patanjali Junior are available in the market in three lakh outlets. Patanjali's oral care market share has been pegged at nearly 2 per cent.

Colgate plans to take away the pricing edge of Patanjali. Vedshakti is priced at ₹50 for a 175 gm pack, almost 30 per cent cheaper than Patanjali Danti Kanti (Regular), which is available in 100 gm packs of ₹40, and ₹75 for a 200 gm pack, throwing a challenge at Patanjali.

Challenges for Patanjali

To keep the momentum going, Patanjali must build a huge support mechanism, specially ensuring constant supply of ingredients needed for its organic formulation. Creating a supply chain for natural ingredients demands huge infrastructure development and huge investment. In contrast, MNCs already have an efficient, low-cost global supply chain in place for chemical ingredients that go into conventional FMCG products. There are no such ready-made solutions for ayurvedic versions.

In fact, this is one of the reasons why Indian FMCG players that enthusiastically adopted the 'herbal' plank have tasted limited success in the past, whether it was Himalaya and Zandu Pharmaceuticals, or Hindustan Unilever, which had to shelve its Ayush rollout. 'Another factor (as to) why herbal products didn't pick up well in the past is because of the prevalence of herbal home remedies. Sourcing of the quality ingredients for consumer products is also tough as well as the scale which is needed to source them,' says Rajat

Wahi, head of consumer markets at KPMG, in a report.

'When you have such an extraordinary growth, you need to build your supply chain for sourcing and procurement, and your vendors need to be compliant. Patanjali is not fully cognizant of the challenges of this. There's no way that you can grow at this pace and have your supply chain grow with you,' *Forbes* quotes Arvind Singhal, chairman of Technopak Advisors, consumer products and retail consultants.[6]

Acquiring a nationwide distribution presence will also require more sophisticated supply chain and inventory management. But at the same time, these additional expenses will have an impact on Patanjali's profits. In FY15, Patanjali Ayurved reported a 23 per cent operating profit margin with a 16 per cent net profit margin. This was fairly comparable with the margins—operating profits at 17–25 per cent—of the listed FMCG firms. But then, listed FMCG players manage these margins after spending 12 to 18 per cent of their sales on advertising and promotion.

'Patanjali Ayurved's products are typically at a 15–30 per cent discount to competing brands which has been possible through its strong sourcing back-end and are even available on Amazon,' says a report.[7] So the challenge now is how Patanjali will accommodate similar spends if it is to continue with its low-price strategy. An Axis Capital report notes that

---

[6]http://www.forbes.com/sites/meghabahree/2016/10/26/indias-baba-ramdev-billionaire-is-not-baba-ramdev/#59d3b1767931
[7]http://smartinvestor.business-standard.com/market/story-332768-storydet-Wish_you_were_listed_Patanjali_Ayurved_CLSA.htm#.WMKGVTuGPIU

Patanjali will find it difficult to increase its market share beyond 5 to 10 per cent because the Ayurveda segment will continue to remain a niche. It also states that Patanjali's strategy of entering multiple categories may challenge management bandwidth.

'The even more burning question is where Patanjali will find the capital needed to bankroll its mega investment plans. In fact, with over 90 per cent of its equity held by Acharya Balkrishna, it isn't even clear how Patanjali has found all the equity for its successes so far. Yes, the MNCs that Ramdev reviles do make huge profits and pay out generous dividends and royalties to their foreign parents. But by virtue of being publicly listed companies in India, multinationals such as Hindustan Unilever or Nestlé India have also contributed to the exchequer and turned many ordinary investors into millionaires. For Patanjali to gain similar credibility, it needs to explore a listing on the public markets too. Not only will that clear the air on the company's funding sources, it may open up one more swadeshi option for Indian investors in FMCG stocks,' states a 9 June 2016 report in the Hindu.[8]

Analysts Vivek Maheshwari and Bhavesh Pravin Shah of CLSA, in a report titled 'Wish you were listed: Patanjali Ayurved'[9], said: 'PAL perhaps lacks most ingredients for building a large-scale consumer goods business, be its negligible advertisement and promotion spends or distribution

---

[8] http://www.thehindubusinessline.com/opinion/columns/a-reality-check-on-patanjali/article8710429.ece

[9] http://www.business-standard.com/article/markets/wish-you-were-listed-patanjali-ayurved-clsa-115082800265_1.html

network. Yet, the brand power of a yoga guru has brought PAL into the top league.'

Through a newspaper report, Rajeev Sharma, CEO of Ormax Rhodium, and ex-national head of planning and strategy at Leo Burnett, offered a piece of advice to Patanjali. Though Sharma believes that Baba Ramdev has brought a credible and popular voice of authority to the ayurvedic segment for the first time, thus fuelling its growth, he said: 'The MNC bashing that Patanjali has indulged in, is good for a few market share points, but this merely scratches the surface of what it can be. Sooner than later, Patanjali will realize that for the larger market, there is a bigger issue as far as the consumer is concerned. It is the wall of scepticism that traditional or Ayurvedic dental products have to scale to be a truly dominant force.'

Ramdev had openly ridiculed his multinational competition. 'It's just the start. *Ab tak Colgate ka toh gate khul gaya, Nestlé ka toh panchhi urne wala hai, Pantene ka toh pant gila hone wala hai; aur do saal me, Unilever ka lever kharab ho jayega* (By now, Colgate's gate has opened; Nestlé's bird has flown [a reference to Nestlé's India Ltd's logo], Pantene's [a shampoo brand by Procter & Gamble India] pants are going to get wet, and in two years, Unilever's lever will fail),' Ramdev said on 27 April 2016 at a press conference in Delhi. Perhaps realizing that these claims are too ambitious to be true, he later told *India Today*: 'Those lines are said in jest. My goal is not to harm anyone. I want draw my line longer, not to shorten anyone's. But yes, this challenge should alert them not to cheat customers and overprice.'

Then with a serious note he added: 'This is also a warning to all companies, including the Indians. One must have world-class infrastructure, research and product. One must be responsible for what the group produces, whether it's owned by a sadhu or by anyone. If Sri Sri Ravi Shankar is producing something, he must have complete knowledge of every product. Otherwise, he must stop. For every product produced by Patanjali, I own moral and spiritual responsibility.'

It's clear that Baba has eyes on not only the ones he is challenging but also on those who could be his challengers. But he has some kind words for his desi competitors. 'Till my last breath, I will not target any Indian company. If competition occurs between the brands by itself, that's all right, but we won't actively pursue them. Yes, we will help control their prices for the benefit of the consumers. We'll show them the way to do it; that is the work of a sanyasi,' he said in an interview to *The Indian Express*.[10]

Ramdev may soon face competition from his own breed of babas. Following Patanjali's 'spectacular' success, Edelweiss Securities Ltd expects other spiritual gurus, including Sri Sri Ravi Shankar, Guru Ram Rahim Singh, and Sadhguru Jaggi Vasudev, 'to go the Patanjali way,' analyst Abneesh Roy and his colleagues said in a report in March 2016. Sant Shri Asharamji Bapu Ashram, Sri Aurobindo Ashram and BAPS

---

[10]http://indianexpress.com/article/india/india-news-india/baba-ramdev-is-india-only-a-place-for-pak-artists-to-earn-crores-and-not-comment-on-terror-3727920/

Swaminarayan Sanstha are other organizations that not only cater to the spiritual needs of millions of followers, but are also emerging as suppliers of fast-moving consumer goods, the Edelweiss report said. Shankar's Sri Sri Ayurveda, in particular, is showing 'renewed aggression' as it rides on the brand equity of its founder, whose 'Art of Living' movement has 370 million followers worldwide. Sri Sri Ayurveda is beginning to use mass media, point-of-sale advertising and online retailing. In October, the group began selling a range of ayurvedic health drinks under the Ojasvita brand and signed Olympic silver medallist P.V. Sindhu to help promote it in a market dominated by GlaxoSmithKline's Horlicks brand.

Meanwhile, there have been some damaging media reports regarding the quality of Patanjali products. According to Ramdev, Patanjali has more than 200 scientists who research, develop its products and ensure quality. Amit Sachdeva, who wrote the HDFC report, also said, 'About 85 per cent of all production is done in-house.' However, a report in *Mint* claimed: 'Patanjali claims to make natural ghee (clarified butter) from cow milk. At the factory, pasteurized unsalted butter produced by the Karnataka Co-operative Milk Products Federation Ltd was being mixed with local cow milk to produce ghee. The aloe vera unit is a processing and packaging unit, which was using pulp supplied by Dhandev Resorts and Health Care Pvt. Ltd (a Jaisalmer-based company owned by Roop Ram, an Indian National Congress leader). Patanjali claims that it has its own aloe vera plantations for making aloe vera juice. And contrary to

Ramdev's claims, Patanjali outsources manufacturing of some products like other packaged consumer products companies do. For instance, biscuits are made by Delhi-based Sona Biscuits (that also sells biscuits under Sobisco brand) and juices by a bunch of companies, including GK Dairy and Milk Products Pvt. Ltd (this company also sells products under the Gopalji brand). Patanjali's juice products, which Ramdev claims to be natural, contain added sugar, water and required preservatives. Haridwar-based Aakash Yog Health Products Ltd manufactures noodles for Patanjali. Aakash used to make noodles for HUL's Knorr brand, till recently.'

As expected, Ramdev rubbished such reports and claims that quality and genuinenss are the two factors which have made his products popular across the globe. 'People did not accept my form of yoga because of any advertisement. They saw the benefits. It's the same for my products. They stand for the credibility that I have built over the years. I must commit to consumers that 99 per cent of Patanjali's products are manufactured in-house. Only some work was awarded on contract to others, a practice followed by MNCs and others in India and rest of the world. We never compromise on quality of products and we sell only those products, which I personally use. Some people or groups with vested interests are spreading these baseless rumours.'

～♨

The Future of Patanjali

With an aim to boost his business and meet growing demands for Patanjali products in domestic and international markets, Ramdev is opening six new production units—two in Uttar Pradesh and one each in Maharashtra, Madhya Pradesh, Assam and Jammu. These units are scheduled to be operational by end of 2017. It also has expansion plans in Andhra Pradesh, West Bengal and Karnataka, besides establishing subsidiary units in a number of places, as part of supply chain.

'Now, we are opening food parks in Nagpur, Noida, Tezpur and Indore. We can cover the entire country through this. We plan to expand to southern India too. We would like to have small units everywhere. We can work on a large scale in Andhra Pradesh and Karnataka,' said Balkrishna.

'We will give employment to more than 5 lakh youths in five years and would benefit more than 5 crore farmers. Patanjali has benefitted more than 1 crore farmers and will further benefit women and entrepreneurs by expanding our business in textile sector in days to come,' said Ramdev.

In Uttar Pradesh, former Chief Minister Akhilesh Yadav laid the foundation of the food and herbal park in Greater Noida, alongside Yamuna Expressway, to be constructed on 455 acres with an investment of ₹1,666.80 crore. The ambitious project aims at integrating farmers with the markets and the wider world. It is also setting up a 150–200 megawatt solar power unit in Uttar Pradesh.

The Greater Noida plant will be an international food park that will cater to overseas and domestic markets as well. It is slated to manufacture all major products. It is expected to act as a hub given its location in the NCR region, which has proximity to the airport and dry ports. The plant, at full capacity, will produce goods worth ₹25,000 crore annually. It is expected to generate around 10,000 direct jobs that can benefit nearly 50,000 families.

'We have decided to start operations on the site from March 2018. We aim to invest ₹1,600 crore in this project, which will benefit around 50,000 local farmers. We will procure the supply of milk and other raw material for food products such as ghee, oil, etc., from farmers,' reads a Patanjali press release. Patanjali will also invest ₹1,600 crore in another project it is going to set up in the Lalitpur district of Uttar Pradesh.

Ramdev's company will be setting up its biggest unit on a 40-lakh square feet area at Mihan in Nagpur, which will be bigger than its first unit at Haridwar and biggest in the country. The total investment in Nagpur, which also happens to be the headquarters of RSS, will be to the tune of ₹1,000 crore with a potential of providing employment opportunities to 10,000 to 15,000 youths from Maharashtra. The food-processing unit at Nagpur will export products to the US and other international destinations while rest of the units will cater to the domestic demand.

Down south, Patanjali group plans to set up a mega food park in Andhra Pradesh. The group has approached the state government for allotment of 200 acres in north coastal Andhra Pradesh for the purpose. Patanjali group is also setting up a similar park in Nellore district where it has bought about 150 acres. Besides the two mega parks, it proposes to set up 66 food processing units in the state over the next three years. 'We hope that the two mega food parks will bring in an investment of about ₹700 crore, and generate 10,000 jobs,' Y.S. Prasad, CEO of Andhra Pradesh Food Processing Society said in a newspaper interview. Andhra Pradesh government has offered ₹50 crore incentives to mega food parks, apart from extending the benefits under Central government-assisted schemes for processing units.

In Assam, where BJP came to power for the first time in 2016, Patanjali has started work on a mega food park in Sonitpur district with an investment of ₹1,200 crore. It's not far from the area in Assam where Ramdev first distributed his medicine for malaria. Spread across 150 acres, it will generate 4,000 direct jobs for local youth, claims Ramdev. However, before generating jobs, this project has generated controversies.

An elephant that fell at a construction site of the food park died and the state government has registered a police case against 'unknown persons'.

'Something which shouldn't have happened has happened. I have directed my department to register a police case to probe the reasons that led to the elephant's death,' Forest Minister Pramila Rani Brahma had said to journalists, 'I have heard this area is frequented by wild elephants. If the land was allotted to Patanjali despite this knowledge, it is unfortunate. Protective measures should have been taken.'

According to Ramdev and Balkrishna, the focus for expansion over the next few years will revolve around broadly six areas—natural medicine, natural cosmetics, natural dairy products and food, natural cattle feed and feed supplements, bio-fertilizers and bio-pesticides and natural indigenous seeds. The duo claims that Patanjali will be spending ₹500 crore on research across their four verticals—food, cosmetics, herbal and home care. It will also invest ₹750 crore in research on Ayurveda.

Beyond research, the company is all set to enter new domains. 'Patanjali's plans involve getting into the garment sector, especially "Swadeshi" jeans that the youth of the country are demanding. It also wants to enter [the markets of] edible oil and home products like toilet cleaners. There's a huge vacuum in the market for quality products and Patanjali enjoys enormous public loyalty that ensures success for all our products,' Ramdev said in an interview.

By mid-2017, Patanjali will launch the swadeshi jeans under the brand name 'Paridhaan' with an initial investment of ₹1,000 crore. 'I don't have [any] objection to wearing jeans or skirts but it should be swadeshi. That's what Mahatma

Gandhi taught us,' says Ramdev. Along with jeans, it will also manufacture workout wear, including gym and yoga attire.

'The idea of the apparel brand started with some followers asking me for Patanjali yoga wear. Then we thought, why not a whole range of dresses—'Paridhaan'—for everyone? If we are fighting to achieve economic independence for our country from multinationals by promoting indigenous and natural products, we should also be in the garments market,' he told *The Telegraph*.

And the Baba has already picked up his rivals. 'I'm sorry. I have bad news for Nike, Adidas, Puma and Reebok. They will soon face the toughest competition in their history,' he says. Another MNC, which will face the Ramdev challenge, will be Johnson & Johnson as Patanjali has also launched a baby care product line called 'Shishu Care'.

On 5 January, coinciding with the 22nd birth anniversary of Divya Pharmacy, Ramdev launched seven varieties of edible oil—rice bran, groundnut, soyabean, sunflower, sesame, canola and virgin coconut oil. It's already a market player in mustard oil. 'All the oils will be physically processed— you can call them virgin oils—with no chemicals involved,' Ramdev declared in Haridwar.

Patanjali Refined, as the oil label is being called, is eyeing sales of ₹20,000 crore in the next three years, and is expected be one of the big contributors to the target of ₹50,000 crore in 2020 that the company has set for itself. The total market size of edible oil in India is around ₹125,000 crore currently and it's growing at 7–8 per cent annually.

Though, at the moment, production units have been

taken on lease, Ramdev claims that self-owned manufacturing units will come up too. Patanjali Refined will be rolled out nationally across one million retail touch-points.

Ramdev also plans to venture into the beauty care segment. Of its total product lines, about 100 are cosmetic products. According to Patanjali, the herbal ingredients in the cosmetic range will be the unique selling proposition. The Patanjali unit at Haridwar is on course to double its shampoo production to 10 lakh bottles.

'We have a ready market of 500 tons of soap per day which we are not able to meet. Similarly, demand has shot up for products such as dish washing liquid and face wash. Our six new units across the country (UP, Maharashtra, MP, Assam and J&K) will meet such demand,' Ramdev said in Haridwar.

Patanjali has also drawn up an ambitious strategy to disrupt India's packaged rice market, which is currently dominated by brands such as India Gate, Kohinoor, Best Basmati and Daawat. Research firm Euromonitor has valued the market at ₹22,000 crore and said it will grow at a CAGR of 11 per cent till 2020.

In September 2016, Patanjali acquired R.H. Agro's rice mill in Sonipat, Haryana, for ₹70 crore and has taken four other rice mills across the country on exclusive lease, to actualize its plan to launch eighteen packaged rice brands. Patanjali has been currently selling three variants of packaged rice—silver, gold and diamond. It meets its procurement needs by buying finished rice and packaging it at its Haridwar facility. The new mills will not only give the FMCG company the capability of producing 3.2 lakh tonnes of finished rice a year from paddy, but it will also allow it to produce region-specific rice variants that it plans to sell locally and export as well. 'We have partnered with thousands of rice farmers in many regions of the country to produce traditional variants,' says Balkrishna.

The rice brands will be made available in fifty SKUs (stock keeping unit) of various sizes. Prices will range between ₹67 for one kilo of Sona Masoori Steam and ₹2,100 for 25 kg of Lashkari (kolam), said the company. Senior executives at Patanjali said its new rice variants will have a shelf life of two years, which is double that of the brands available in the market. 'Some of our variants will also take less time to cook than competing brands,' claims Patanjali.

Other than the mill in Sonipat, which will process basmati, Patanjali has leased two mills in Madhya Pradesh to process the pusa variety. Another mill in Telangana will produce the lightweight aromatic Sona Masuri to cater to the markets in the South, while a mill in Fazilka, Punjab, will process rice grains that are grown in the North. Around 150 varieties of rice are currently grown in the country, industry estimates show.

Perhaps, I can claim a little credit in Patanjali's venture into rice production. Whenever I have met him, I have always egged the yoga guru to start selling multiple types of rice from across the country. He is yet to promise me that he would make Assamese Joha rice available in every nook and corner of the country, but I have hopes.

To be future ready, Patanjali has further drawn up ₹5,000

Baba Ramdev is the face of Patanjali Ayurved and the brand ambassador of Haryana, and is one of the most popular faces of yoga.
Courtesy: Bandeep Singh/*India Today*

Ramdev popularized yoga as an instant thirty-minute drill to cure multiple ailments.
Courtesy: The Yellow Coin Communication.

While Ramdev is the bundle of restless energy, Balkrishna is the epitome of calmness.
Courtesy: The Yellow Coin Communication.

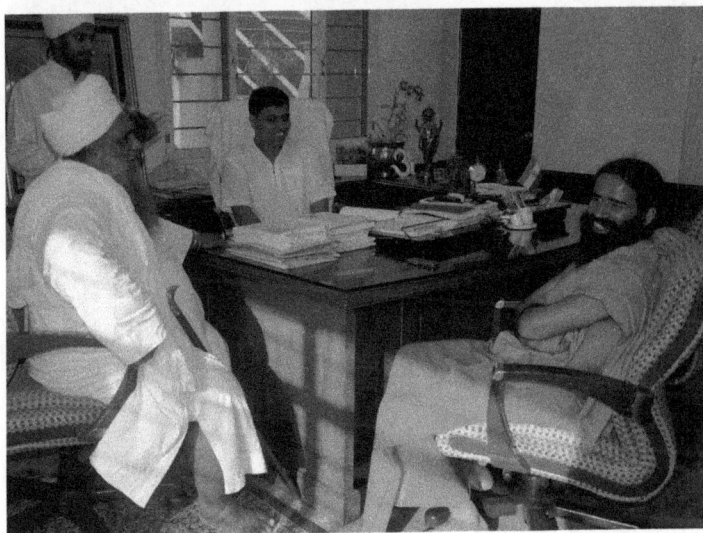

Acharya Balkrishna is the hands-on CEO of Patanjali.
Courtesy: The Yellow Coin Communication.

If Ramdev is the public face of Patanjali, Balkrishna is its meticulous
planner and executioner.
Courtesy: Bandeep Singh/*India Today*

Baba Ramdev at one of the factory units of Patanjali Ayruved in Haridwar.
Courtesy: Bandeep Singh/*India Today*

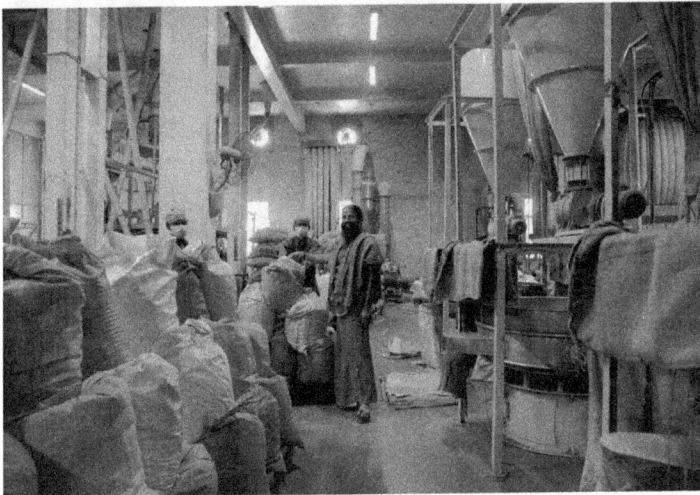

Ramdev at his Haridwar factory.
Courtesy: Bandeep Singh/*India Today*

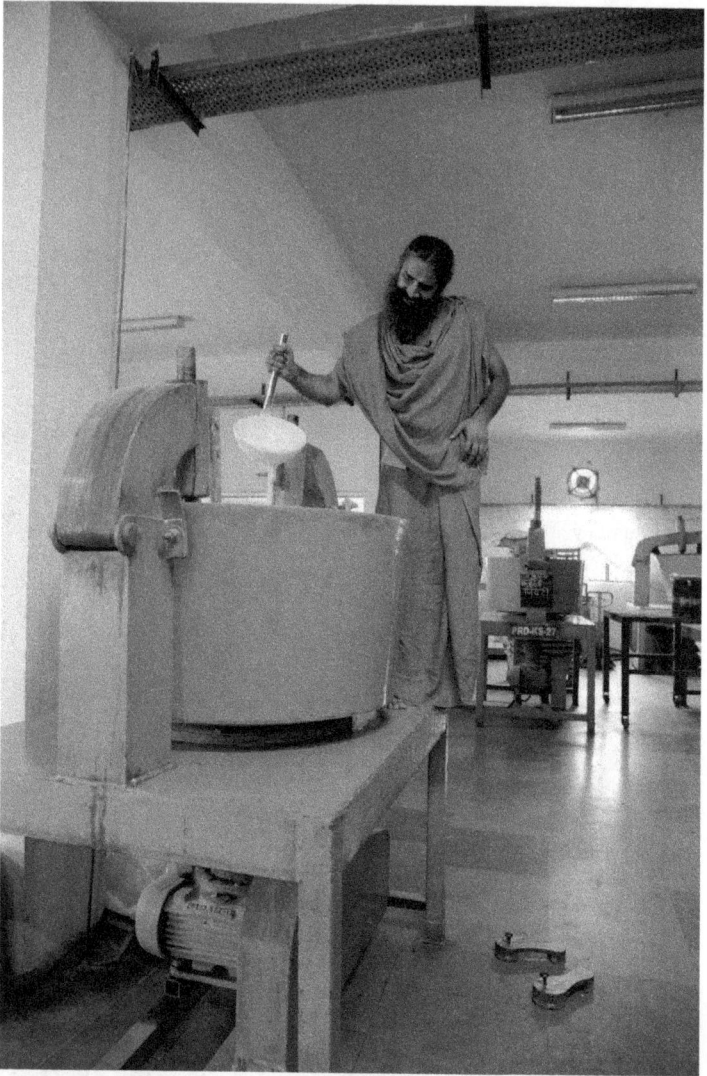

Patanjali is a mix of adhyatyamikta (spirituality) and adhunikta (modernity), according to Baba Ramdev.
Courtesy: Bandeep Singh/*India Today*

At one of the acharyakulam schools in Haridwar.
Courtesy: Bandeep Singh/*India Today*

Ramdev: 'It is high time that the cow, which is our mother, got due attention.'
Courtesy: Bandeep Singh/ *India Today*

Since 1993, when Ramdev began teaching yoga to only two men, his followers have grown manifold and across the globe.
Courtesy: The Yellow Coin Communication.

The number of Ramdev's yoga camps and people attending those camps has continued to increase.
Courtesy: The Yellow Coin Communication.

Be it politics or Patanjali, he is always seen leading from the front.
Courtesy: The Yellow Coin Communication.

Bollywood actor and writer Kader Khan was admitted to Ramdev's Patanjali Yogpeeth in Haridwar in 2015.
Courtesy: The Yellow Coin Communication.

Despite wearing his Hindu pride on his sleeve, Ramdev has refrained from giving religious discourse.
Courtesy: The Yellow Coin Communication.

Acharya Balkrishna, originally hailing from Nepal, with the country's Prime Minister Pushpa Kamal Dahal 'Prachanda'.
Courtesy: The Yellow Coin Communication.

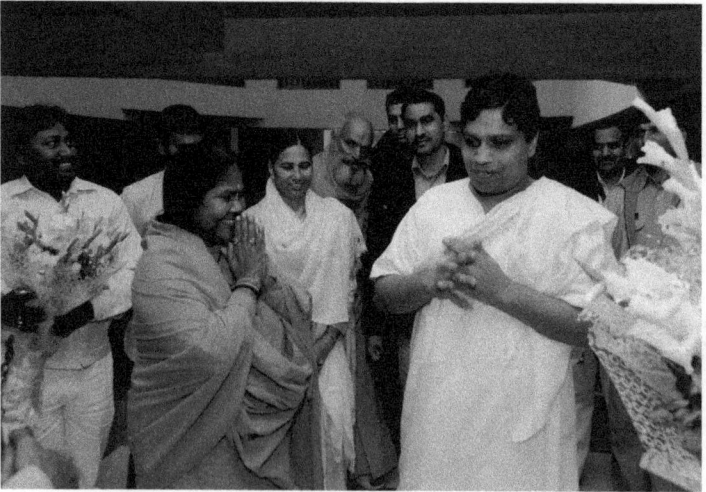

Acharya Balkrishna with Sadhvi Niranjan Jyoti, Minister of State for Food Processing Industries.
Courtesy: The Yellow Coin Communication.

BJP President Amit Shah is a follower of Baba Ramdev's yogic and Ayurvedic discourse.
Courtesy: The Yellow Coin Communication.

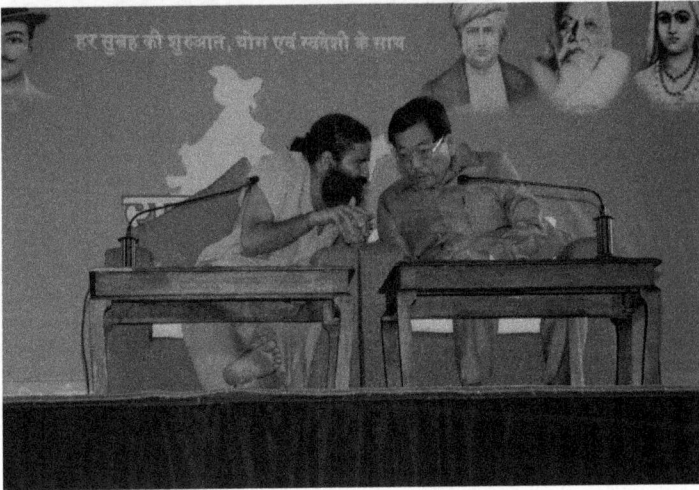

Baba Ramdev with Pawan Kumar Chamling, Chief Minister of Sikkim.
Courtesy: The Yellow Coin Communication.

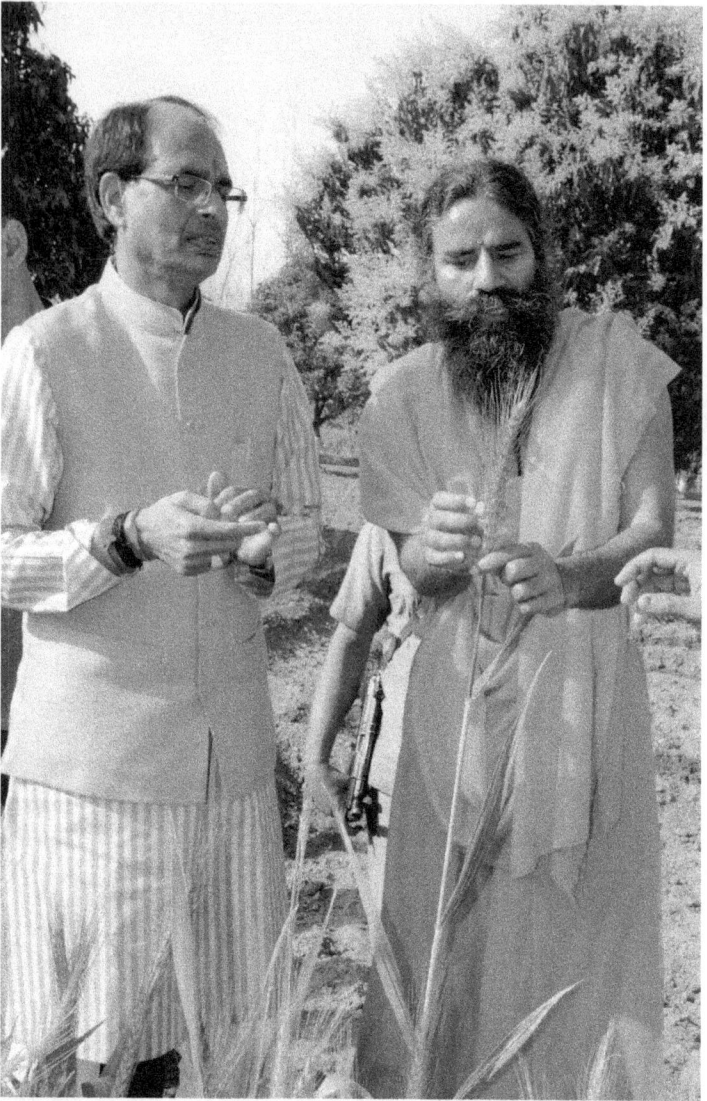

Madhya Pradesh Chief Minister Shivraj Singh has been a long-time supporter of Baba Ramdev.
Courtesy: The Yellow Coin Communication.

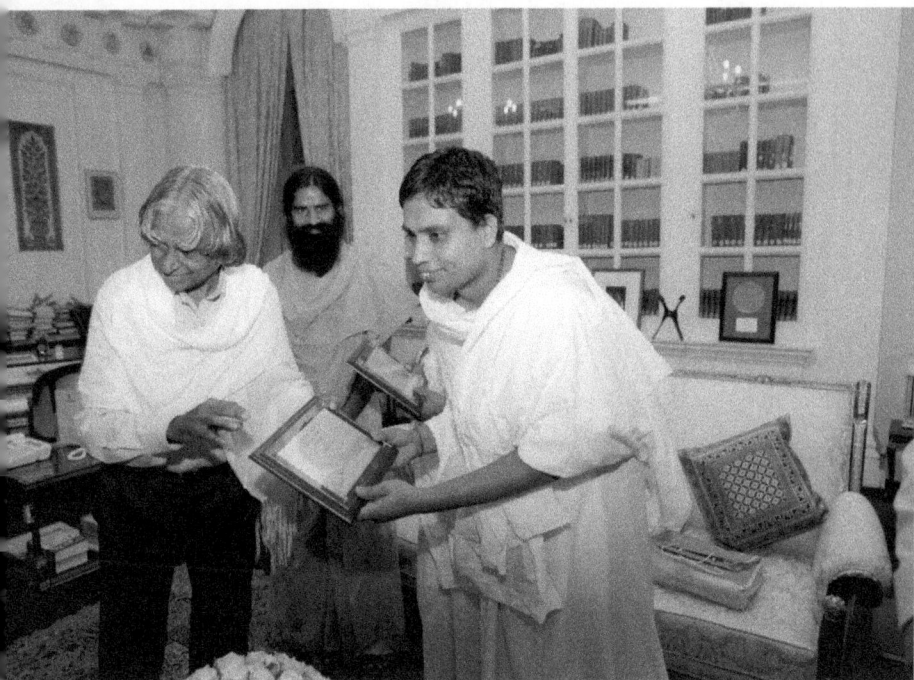

Acharya Balkrishna and Baba Ramdev with former President A.P.J. Abdul Kalam.
Courtesy: The Yellow Coin Communication.

On 7 September 2013, Ramdev had said that he would not support BJP unless it declared Narendra Modi (seen here with Acharya Balkrishna) as the Prime Ministerial candidate of the party.
Courtesy: The Yellow Coin Communication.

crore capital expenditure plan for 2017–18. According to the Axis Capital report, Patanjali's expansion plan is based on a two-phase pull model as compared to a push model used by its FMCG rivals. In the first phase, the focus is given to demand creation through dedicated channels in a select geography. In its next phase, armed with a sizable customer base, the focus shifts to expanding general trade.

The company will also set up 1,000 mega stores of over 2,000 square feet each in select cities, as part of its effort to push margins higher up to around 19 per cent, the Axis report added.

The company had announced in a statement that over the next year, Patanjali will increase its retail presence through 4,000 distributors, more than 10,000 company-owned outlets, 100 Patanjali-branded stores and supermarkets.

GOING GLOBAL

Ramdev has also announced that he is set to launch Patanjali products globally and has decided to set up its units in foreign markets including Nepal, Bangladesh and some African nations. He has gone on record saying that he would not hesitate in setting up Patanjali units in Pakistan and Afghanistan, if he gets the required permit. 'We've set up factories in Nepal and Bangladesh and are now approaching African nations. Our products have reached West Asia and are popular even in countries like Saudi Arabia,' says Ramdev. He has also stated that Patanjali has already entered Azerbaijan, which has 90 per cent Muslim population, claiming that a top industrialist there has shown interest in his products.

And it's not just Middle East or developing countries, he has eyes on First World regions such as the US and Europe. He is, however, quick to distinguish Patanjali from other multinational brands emphasizing that his motto is not to just make money in different parts of the globe. 'Profits earned would be used in those countries for development, and won't be ploughed back to India,' he says.

❧

POWER AND POLITICS

The Political Animal

In 2007, when Ramdev started Patanjali Yogpeeth, fifteen chief ministers attended the event. Yet when Assam Chief Minister Sarbananda Sonowal invited the yoga guru to his swearing-in ceremony, Ramdev politely declined. 'As a principle, I stay away from such political events,' he said.

Ramdev's disenchantment with politics stems from the fact that unlike his yoga and corporate adventure, his intermittent political forays have remained largely unsuccessful and on several occasions have dented his credibility. But he remains unfazed. 'When I led my political campaign, I did not care for my reputation. Rather I staked my reputation. I did it because it was for the welfare of the society,' he told me.

In an earlier interview, he justified his presence in politics: 'Apart from being an ascetic, I am also a citizen of India and I am answerable to my country. That is why whenever there is a political crisis, I should do what I feel is best for the country. Politics is not my full-time occupation. In 2010, I announced a political party, as the country had come to a political standstill. I'm just a man from a village and have no political ambitions. Like they would say in my village, Sonia Gandhi *ne meri koi bhains thodi na khol rakhi hai,* which means we have no animosity against her. As far as the question of a political alternative goes, when I first started my movement in 2009, there was no strong political alternative and that is when I said there needs to be a respectable political institution in place, something I believe in till today.'

His political campaigns have largely revolved around two core issues—swadeshi pride and corruption/black money. On 5 January 2009, along with Rajiv Dixit, a controversial figure who claims to have been a scientist and also doubled up as an Ayurveda expert and economist, Ramdev started 'Bharat Swabhiman Andolan'—a national campaign for restoring India's pride. The initial targets were MNCs and Cola giants, which were compared to toilet cleaners. And then a series of scams—2G, CWG, coal, Adarsh—broke out against the incumbent Congress-led UPA government at the Centre, helping Ramdev's anti-corruption slogan gain traction.

In 2010, Ramdev announced that Bharat Swabhiman Andolan would be converted into a political party and he would field candidates in all 543 Lok Sabha constituencies in next general elections. In 2010, Yoga Guru Baba Ramdev announced his entry into politics by naming his party— the Bharat Swabhiman, but insisted he wouldn't contest elections. 'I will join politics to cleanse the system,' said Ramdev.

He said his party would field candidates in all the 543 Lok Sabha seats in a bid to build a corruption-free India. 'We will have 7–10 lakh members in every district in a year or two. The next general election would be a watershed event when all the corrupt politicians will be wiped out. One of the main objectives of the movement is to end corruption and to bring back more than ₹300 lakh crore of black money from abroad for the country's development,' he said.

In his initial journey in politics, he joined hands with the team members of India Against Corruption led by social activist Anna Hazare and the then RTI activist and now Delhi Chief Minister Arvind Kejriwal. In fact, on the suggestion of Kiran Bedi, who is now lieutenant governor of Puducherry, Anna Hazare and Kejriwal visited Ramdev at his ashram seeking his help in their mission against corruption. Ramdev had already launched his agitation against corruption, especially against the CWG scam, on 2 September 2010 from Dwarka in Gujarat and continued the first phase of his Bharat Swabhiman Yatra till 3 November 2010. On 14 November 2010, Ramdev, along with Kejriwal and eight others, signed a petition demanding the arrest of Suresh Kalmadi, the then president of Indian Olympic Association and head of the Commonwealth Organising Committee on charges of corruption. But Dixit's mysterious death in Bhillai in Madhya Pradesh in November 2010, and allegations of Ramdev's involvement in his death also put an end to the dream of a political party. Dixit's hold over certain people even after six years of his death is intriguing. In my story in *India Today*, I described him as a controversial and mysterious personality. Though I maintain minimal presence on Twitter, I was trolled, received death threat and there were incessant calls to my office demanding apology, and some even threatened a dharna at Jantar Mantar. All these came from self-proclaimed followers of Dixit.

However Ramdev's crusade against corruption did not end there. On 27 February 2011, Ramdev held a rally in Delhi's Ramlila Maidan which was attended by Anna Hazare, Arvind Kejriwal, Kiran Bedi (then IAC member who later fought polls in Delhi as BJP chief ministerial candidate against Kejriwal, and is now lieutenant governor of Puducherry), lawyer Ram Jethmalani (Modi supporter turned critic), Hindu think-tank K.M. Govindacharya and Dr Subramanian Swami (now BJP Rajya Sabha member). The date was significant as it was the death anniversary of Chandra Shekhar Azad and also Swami Dayanand Saraswati Jayanti that day. After the rally, they submitted a memorandum to President Pratibha Patil demanding a strong anti-corruption law in the form of a Lokpal Act to deal with the menace. They also demanded that the government take effective steps to bring back money stashed by Indian nationals in banks abroad. The memorandum, under the aegis of the 'Bharat Swabhiman Trust', was reportedly signed by thirty lakh people. This is where Anna Hazare declared he would go on an indefinite fast from 5 April if the Prime Minister did not initiate action by that March to enact a stronger Lokpal Bill.

This declaration was made suddenly and Ramdev was not even consulted on this. The yoga guru was hurt by this attempt by Kejriwal and his friends to usurp the anti-corruption movement. 'I did not want credit, but transparency,' said Ramdev. But gradually the distance between Team Anna Hazare and Ramdev grew as both became increasingly suspicious of each other. While Ramdev was uncomfortable with the fact that Team Anna was hijacking his battle against corruption, IAC members saw him as a BJP agent. The final blow was when Ramdev made comments about nepotism in the formation of the civil society team involved in the drafting of Jan Lokpal Bill, as the father and son duo of Shanti Bhushan and Prashant Bhushan were part of it. Also, he kept changing his stand on various provisions of the Lokpal Bill. On 31 May 2011, Baba Ramdev said in Madhya Pradesh's Sehore district that the prime minister and CJI should not come under the ambit of Lokpal given that these posts were highly dignified. The next day he did a volte-face. 'I did not say that the proposed Lokpal Bill should not cover the prime minister and CJI as their posts are highly dignified,' he told reporters after ending his 1 lakh km 'Bharat Swabhiman Yatra' which was done to 'awaken people about corruption and black money'.

On 4 June 2011 he sat on an indefinite fast to launch his 'Bhrashtachar Mitao Satyagraha' from Delhi's Ramlila Maidan. He had three demands from the UPA government—recover black money stashed away in foreign banks, ban high-denomination currency notes and award death sentence to the corrupt. When he arrived in Delhi on the evening of 3 June, four senior cabinet ministers led by the then finance minister and now President Pranab Mukherjee went to meet him at the airport to try and persuade him to call off his fast. Baba did not relent.

Tehelka published a nasty account[11] of Ramdev, who was too flattered by his own popularity as a yoga guru and assumed that he would walk away with all the glory as the chief crusader against corruption. An excerpt:

> In fact, during the entire course of events that unfolded that particular week when the drama shifted from Delhi's Ramlila Maidan to Haridwar, it was surprising to see ND Tiwari, said to be his original patron when the latter was chief minister, having to wait ninety minutes to meet Ramdev. And despite Tiwari's age, he had to climb to the second floor to meet the Baba, who did not oblige him by descending [down] the stairs.

One day later, the government changed its mind and launched a midnight police operation on the agitators—mostly members of Bharat Swabhiman Andolan—and Ramdev was also arrested while trying to escape in disguise wearing a woman's salwar kameez. He was flown back in a helicopter to Haridwar where he continued his fast unto death. But he had to abort his fast and campaign as his health deteriorated seriously within four days.

Ramdev makes some face-saving attempts by giving his own account of the disgraceful end to his rally. 'Had I not stopped my people from reacting, the brutal police action

---

[11]http://www.tehelka.com/2011/06/babas-black-sheep-and-the-golden-fleece/

would have left many dead as had happened in Jallianwala Bagh. Policemen thrashed even women and children. They used tear gas shells and attacked without warning. I escaped by wearing a woman's dress and hiding behind a wall. I would not have been caught had it not been for some women accompanying me telling me not to worry, as there were no policemen nearby. A policeman who heard this comment immediately arrested me. They even tried to strangle him with the dupatta.'

On 20 September 2011, Ramdev started the second phase of his Bharat Swabhiman Yatra from Rani Lakshmibai Qila in Jhansi. In March 2012, he again joined hands with Team Anna, which had also lost much of its initial sheen, and announced that they would jointly fight for a strong Lokpal Bill and to bring back black money stashed in foreign banks. Hazare even went to meet Ramdev in the latter's ashram in Haridwar. On 25 March, they held a day-long hunger strike at Jantar Mantar. On 3 June 2013, he began the third phase of his Bharat Swabhiman Yatra from Delhi's Jantar Mantar. On 9 August 2012, he sat for a three-day fast demanding immediate action to enact a strong Lokpal Bill and steps to bring back black money at the same Ramlila Maidan from where he had been unceremoniously evicted a year ago. This time he took a softer stance expressing his eagerness to start a dialogue with the government on a range of issues. He wanted a change in the process of appointing Election Commissioners, CAG, CVC and CBI directors. When journalists questioned the absence of Team Anna during his fast, he was diplomatic with his answer:

'We are with Anna's social agenda but not with the team.'

On 7 September 2013, at Delhi's Jantar Mantar, he declared that he would not support BJP if Narendra Modi had not been declared the prime ministerial candidate of the party. Six days later, Modi was announced PM candidate of the saffron party. The same day, Ramdev started the fourth phase of his Bharat Swabhiman Yatra from Delhi. 'I had decided not to return to Haridwar till I could not make Modi the PM of India,' he said. Ramdev returned to Haridwar on 18 May 2014, two days after results were declared of the Lok Sabha elections. Modi-led BJP won a record 282 seats.

Web of Influence

Narendra Modi: Backed by Ramdev as BJP's prime ministerial candidate. Reportedly, he also has direct access to the Prime Minister.

Arun Jaitley: When the nation was debating intolerance of the right wing, Ramdev said that Modi and Jaitley were the biggest victims of intolerance. The Enforcement Directorate this year also closed a case of alleged FEMA violation slapped on Ramdev by the UPA government.

Rajnath Singh: Home Ministry under Singh has provided Ramdev with Z-category security; the CBI in 2014 filed closure report on the case investigating the mysterious disappearance of Ramdev's guru in 2007.

Amit Shah: The BJP president is a follower of Baba's yogic and aurvedic discourse.

Nitin Gagdkari: One of his ardent followers; he was instrumental in getting Maharashtra government sign a deal with Patanjali Yogpeeth recently.

Manohar Lal Khattar: The Haryana CM who is an RSS pracharak has made Baba the brand ambassador of the state and even offered him a cabinet rank.

Shivraj Singh Chouhan: A long-time supporter, the Madhya Pradesh CM observed a 24-hour fast in support of the satyagarha launched by Baba Ramdev in June 2011 on repatriation of black money and to protest the police action against the protesters in Delhi.

Devendra Fadnavis: Close to the yoga guru, he also expressed strong views on 'Bharat Mata Ki Jai' slogan. While Ramdev threatened to behead those who did not chant the slogan, Fadnavis said that those unwilling to say 'Bharat Mata ki Jai' have no right to stay in the country.

Sarbananda Sonowal: The Assam CM who was backed by RSS as a CM candidate invited Ramdev to his oath-taking ceremony. But Baba politely declined.

Arun Kumar: Ramdev consulted this JNU professor, who is an AAP supporter, for long hours before raising the black money issue.

Arvind Kejriwal: Ramdev joined hands with Arvind Kejriwal during Anna Hazare-led India Against Corruption movement; but now spares no opportunity to take a dig at Kejriwal.

Anna Hazare: Ramdev was initially a part of Hazare's anti-corruption movement but later started his own agitation demanding repatriation of black money; the two maintain cordial contact.

Pranab Mukherjee: He was one of the four cabinet ministers who went to meet Ramdev at Delhi airport on 4 June 2011 to persuade the yoga guru to call off his satyagraha at Ramlila Maidan in Delhi. Ramdev always has words of praise for the President.

Hagrama Mohilary: The CEO of Bodoland Territorial Council has offered 750 acre land to Patanjali Yogpeeth to set up a university and gaushala. Mohilary's Bodoland People's Front (BPF) is now an ally of BJP in Assam.

H.R. Nagendra: Prime Minister Modi's yoga guru, along with Ramdev and Sri Sri Ravi Shankar, is part of the quality control council that issues certificates to yoga trainers in the country.

Kader Khan: Bollywood actor and writer Kader Khan was admitted to Ramdev's Patanjali Yogpeeth in Haridwar in October 2015. The seventy-nine-year-old was suffering from several ailments including diabetes.

Kirron Kher: The BJP MP sought Ramdev's blessings before starting her poll campaign in 2014 Lok Sabha elections.

Shilpa Shetty: The Bollywood actor shared stage with Ramdev in Mumbai showing their yoga skills together.

Aamir Khan: When Aamir Khan said that his wife was thinking of leaving the country because of intolerance, Ramdev countered saying that if there had been intolerance Kiran could not have married Aamir.

Salman Khan: Baba Ramdev criticized Salman Khan's selection as brand ambassador for the Indian contingent at Rio Olympics. In 2011, following Ramdev's eviction from Ramlila Maidan in Delhi, Salman had said: 'Everybody has to follow the law of the land. My baba (father) is at home, industry's baba is Sanju Baba and then there is Sai Baba.'

Shah Rukh Khan: When Shah Rukh Khan expressed his concern over growing intolerance in the country, Ramdev asked him to return his Padmashree.

Sachin Tendulkar: He felicitated Sachin at Patanjali Yogpeeth when the Master Blaster completed twenty years in international cricket. In 2012, he demanded Bharat Ratna for Sachin Tendulkar. But when the cricket legend was made a Rajya Sabha member by the UPA government, Ramdev said that Congress was using Tendulkar to salvage the sinking ship.

Hema Malini: The BJP MP and actor endorses Patanjali biscuits.

Sushil Kumar: The wrestler endorses Patanjali ghee.

Pawan Munjal: Munjal, the head of Hero MotoCorp and Ramdev are both followers of Dayanand Saraswati and share a close friendship.

Kishore Biyani: Ramdev teamed up with Kishore Biyani for distribution of Patanjali products through 243 Future retail outlets owned by Biyani.

Mukesh Ambani: Mukesh Ambani's retail chain Reliance Fresh also distributes Ramdev's products.

Lakshmi Ratan Mittal: The steel baron has hosted Baba in London on several occasions.

Anil Agarwal: The head of Vedanta Group has offered his support to Ramdev's expansion plan for acharyakulams.

Saffron His Robe, Saffron His Politics

Ramdev has always been an ardent supporter of the BJP, and the party even acknowledged the importance of the role played by his countrywide campaign launched ahead of the Lok Sabha polls. An RTI response has revealed that Patanjali Ayurved had donated a sum of ₹1,100,000 on 8 March 2009 to the Bharatiya Janata Party (BJP)—then in the Opposition. In a newspaper interview he claimed that he had predicted six months before the 2014 general elections that the NDA would come to power with nearly 300 seats under Modi's leadership.

'The role played by Ramdev in awakening the voters is similar to the struggles of Mahatma Gandhi and Jayprakash Narayan who stayed away from power. He has no greed for any post... His motto is to strengthen the system. Ramdev's campaign against black money and corruption is similar to those of Mahatma Gandhi and Jayprakash Narayan,' Union Finance Minister Arun Jaitley said in public after BJP's victory in 2014 Lok Sabha elections.

BJP president Amit Shah has publicly thanked the yoga guru for his sustained campaign, which 'contributed significantly to the formation of the Narendra Modi government at the Centre.' Shah did not mince words when he said that all of Ramdev's future endeavours to save Indian languages and literature and to revive yoga and ayurveda, which had the capacity to create a disease-free universe, would get all the support from the government.

The yoga guru has also been extremely generous in his praise of Shah, who is considered to be the most trusted lieutenant of Prime Minister Modi. 'I have seen Amit Shah at close quarters—be it his personal relationships or his political thought. While most people have only seen his hard side, I've met him innumerable times and have never seen him angry. When he speaks about his hopes and aspirations for the country, its past achievements, the direction of its future, he gets lost in his thoughts on how to take it forward. Whenever it comes to the country, he's the softest person, ready to do whatever he can to aid it. For him, politics is not a business; he is not a man chasing any political berth or position. He's committed to an ideal,' Ramdev said in an interactive programme with *The Indian Express.*[12]

It comes as no surprise, therefore, there has been a shower of perks and honour since the BJP came to power at the Centre in 2014 and in several other states afterwards.

---

[12]http://indianexpress.com/article/india/india-news-india/baba-ramdev-is-india-only-a-place-for-pak-artists-to-earn-crores-and-not-comment-on-terror-3727920/

Apart from State governments offering him lands to set up factories, herbal parks, universities, schools and cowsheds, Union Transport Minister Nitin Gadkari even offered him an island in the Andamans to set up a yoga resort.

In November 2014, he was provided with Z-category security by the Central government, taking into account his 'vulnerability to attacks from his opponents'. Ramdev had already been entitled to Z-category security only within the jurisdiction of Uttarakhand as per a decision of the State government.

Nearly a year after he was given Z-category security, the Centre granted paramilitary security cover to his yoga ashram and food park in Haridwar. The Union government deployed 35 armed CISF personnel at Patanjali Food and Herbal Park Private Limited in Haridwar. The move assumes significance as CISF cover is very sparingly granted to the private sector. The food park is the eighth private unit to be guarded by the paramilitary force after it was first mandated for such tasks in the aftermath of the 2008 Mumbai terror attacks. According to officials, the security arrangement costs Patanjali approximately ₹40 lakh per annum. The company also provides all logistical facilities—barracks, armoury and vehicles—to CISF at its own cost. The CISF commando squad is headed by an assistant commandant rank officer and will be deployed on a 'quick reaction team' pattern, which entails stationing them in vantage positions. The routine entry and exit to the food park and the ashram is regulated by the staff and private security hired by Patanjali.

The Modi government has given a big push to

the Patanjali products manufactured by Ramdev's vast business establishment by ordering that these be stocked by the government-run Kendriya Bhandars. In August 2016, the Defence Research and Development Organisation announced that it would tie up with Patanjali Yogpeeth to market herbal supplements and food products made by the organization. Tribal Affairs Minister Jual Oram said that he would collaborate with Ramdev to develop solutions to end malnutrition.

Madhya Pradesh government has decided to put up for sale Patanjali products at fair price shops across the state. 'On the suggestion of Chief Minister Shivraj Singh Chouhan, the products of Baba Ramdev's Patanjali will be put for sale at the fair price shops in the state,' said Minister of State for Cooperatives Vishwas Sarang.

Since the BJP came to power in 2014, the cow has emerged as one of the strongest symbols of divide in India. Some self-styled nationalists have made it their day job to protect the cows from perceived threats from those who don't worship the cows. These people have gone to the extent of physically attacking anyone who they feel can pose a threat to cows. Ramdev certainly doesn't belong to this group, but the cow has often defined his socio-political philosophy and business. 'The cow, which is our mother, has been neglected in our country and it is high time that she got due attention,' says Ramdev.

This Makar Sankranti, Patanjali took its 'Save the Cow' movement to a new height by launching a floor cleaner called Gonyle. Being marketed as an alternate to the disinfectant

Phenyl, it is made from cow urine, eucalyptus oil, pine oil, lemon grass and anti-bacterial herbs. The print advertisement for the product read: 'Stop punishing your hands with chemical-based phenyl. On the occasion of Holy Makar Sankranti, join the movement to save the cow, our holy mother, by embracing Gonyle because mere sloganeering would not suffice to serve this mission. Let's take a small initiative to free our motherland from the stigma of cow slaughtering. Adopt Gonyle and prohibit the cows from being taken to slaughter houses.'

In 2008, the then BJP government in Uttarakhand had given its nod to Patanjali for setting up a cow research institute. In 2017, the state-of-the-art research institute is likely to come up in Haridwar, which will focus on breeding cows. Ramdev claims it will be first of its kind in the country that will breed cows of international standards.

'Our desi breed of cows will give milk up to 60 litres a day. Our goal is to end the monopoly of foreign cattle that presently farmers prefer because of their capacity to produce 50–60 litres of milk a day. Our institute will also double up as the biggest cow shelter in India,' says Ramdev. Patanjali will invest ₹500 crore on four mega shelters for cows across India. And his target is clear even before he has entered the market. 'Why should a Nestlé make profit out of Indian cows?'

As usual he makes concession to the desi brands. 'We have no problem with Amul or any other domestic organization, but who is Nestlé to sell milk in our country considering the farms, farmers and cattle are all ours?' he thunders. Ghee made of cow's milk is one of the largest selling products of Patanjali Ayurved, which currently sources the milk from elsewhere.

And cow is not only about milk. Ramdev claims that the urine of desi cow varieties is capable of curing many kinds of diseases, including cancer. In 2008, Patanjali inked a deal with the Uttarakhand government for procuring 5,000 litres of cow urine every month. According to media reports, more than 2 lakh litres of the same—and an average of 3,000 litres per month at ₹25 per litre—have been supplied to it till now.

But the business of cow urine has also landed Patanjali in trouble. A Tamil Nadu-based Muslim organization, The Tamil Nadu Thowheed Jamat (TNTJ), issued a fatwa against Patanjali products because they allegedly contained cow urine. According to TNTJ, cow urine is 'haram' for Muslims. Balkrishna countered the allegation by stating that only five products made by the firm—Godhan Ark, Sanjivani Vati, Panchgavya Soap, Kayakalp Oil and Shudhi Phenyal—contain cow urine. While Sanjivani Vati is used in the treatment of chronic fever, cold and cough, Panchgavya soap is said to cure skin ailments.

✧

Modi, His Friend

Ramdev's association and tilt towards BJP's philosophy is no secret and the yoga guru has been quite candid about it. He is personally close to several BJP chief ministers—Manohar Lal Khattar, Devendra Fadnavis, Shivraj Singh Chouhan, Raman Singh and Sarbananda Sonowal. During the 2014 Lok Sabha elections, he openly extended support to Narendra Modi's prime ministerial candidature. But in the last two years, though Ramdev's business empire has grown manifold with support from BJP-led government in several states, his relationship with Modi has witnessed several mood swings.

His influence over the Prime Minister could be gauged from the fact that a chance meeting with the yoga guru in a flight to Kolkata earned singer Babul Supriyo not only a BJP ticket but also a ministerial berth later. In February 2015, Modi announced that the income of yoga-related charitable trusts would be exempted from service tax. Ramdev has often praised Modi for what he has done for popularizing yoga. 'AYUSH Ministry has been formed. With his capacity Modiji got international recognition for yoga. Both at international and political level the recognition itself is a huge achievement. Now AYUSH Ministry must devote attention towards research,' said Ramdev.

But in December 2016, when he was asked in an interview if he was happy with the NDA government's performance so far, he said, 'A yogi should neither be happy nor unhappy. I am stuck somewhere in the middle.' Unlike in the past, Baba's praise for Modi was reserved. He was not willing to bat for Modi the way he used to do earlier against all bouncers. In February 2017, at a press conference in Haridwar, he said that he had supported Narendra Modi in the 2014 Lok Sabha elections because Modi was against black money and corruption. If the Congress seeks his support in national interest then he is ready to support it.

His unhappiness with Modi could stem from various developments. The Prime Minister is yet to clear his proposal for a Vedic education board. Modi government has rejected his proposal that Patanjali Yogpeeth be given full control of khadi marketing and management across the country. But his biggest grudge against the Modi government has been its failure to tackle the black money issue the way it had been envisaged by the yoga guru.

In the run up to the 2014 general elections, armed with a research report by JNU professor Arun Kumar and two other papers by Transparency International and Global Financial Integrity, Ramdev raised the issue of black money, a favourite campaign slogan of the then BJP's prime ministerial candidate Narendra Modi. This was not the first time Ramdev has publicly talked about black money in Indian economy. On 27 February 2011, at Delhi's Jantar Mantar, he alleged that Indian nationals had around ₹400 lakh crore in black money, out of which ₹300 lakh crore was stashed in banks abroad. 'I did not estimate the black money amount in the air. I consulted economists such as Kumar for hours and read reports, and then went by the minimum possible amount,' says the yoga guru who loves to talk about economist Joseph Stiglitz and historian Nial Fergusson besides quoting from Kautilya's *Arthashastra*.

His black money narriative has been almost the same as what Prime Minister Modi has often propagated. 'The biggest black money is in mining, followed by gold, land, politics and drugs. If we can get hold of the black money in these five sectors it will hugely benefit the economy, Ramdev often used to prescribe.

It's also true that he has been one of the earliest votaries of cashless economy. 'Cash transaction is not traceable and this leads to black money. Notes of higher denomination should stop. The way banking services have expanded, the transactions should be in cheque, card and draft. We will put pressure (on the government) to get this done,' he had said in 2011. In May 2016, he even claimed that he was seriously thinking about foraying into banking sector.

Though Modi government's first cabinet decision was to form an SIT to investigate and take action on the issue of black money, the follow-up action for next several months did not meet the expectations of Ramdev.

The first sign of discontent came in November 2015. The yoga guru had conceded that the menace of black money had increased under Prime Minister Narendra Modi's government. '*Yeh* (black money) *badhta hi jaa raha hai, yeh multiply hota jaa raha hai* (It keeps increasing). People are stashing black money through tax avoidance as well.'

In May 2016, he attacked the government saying that its inability to bring back black money stashed abroad is leading to 'frustration' among people. In Madhya Pradesh's Ujjain, he said he was silent on the issue of black money because the Central government had failed to get it back to the country from foreign banks. '*Kala dhan nahi aaya isliye is par baat karna band kar diya* (The black money couldn't be brought back, therefore I stopped talking about it).' However, hours later, he appeared to have realized that his comments maybe construed as damaging to the Central government, prompting Ramdev to quickly issue a clarification. According to a TV channel, Ramdev later said that he was confident of the Narendra Modi government bringing back black money to India.

Later in Delhi, he said: 'Wherever I go people say ask me: "Baba has the black money been brought back?" So, there are some issues like the black money which leads to frustration among people (against the Narendra Modi government),' he said.

When reminded about Modi's promise of transferring ₹15 lakh to every Indian's bank account, Ramdev said in an interview to ABP News channel, 'It was for Modiji to decide how soon he intended to fulfil his promise.'

Speaking to India TV, he said: 'It is true that the amount of offshore black money that was expected to be brought back did not come. There is a need to speed up efforts.'

In June 2016, he continued his attack on Modi government. 'Because of lack of effective steps (by the government) on the black money issue, I and people in the country are dissatisfied.'

In January 2017, when reporters in Raipur, where he had gone for a yoga camp, asked him when the country would see the Prime Minister fulfilling his promise of *achhe din* (good days), the baba quipped: 'Practice yoga'.

'No politician or political party can bring *achhe din*. One who practises yoga will be able to bring *achhe din*. Yoga can turn every day into *achhe din*. We will have to work ourselves to get the feeling of *achhe din*. And for this, perform yoga in the morning and later do hard work during the day.'

Despite all these public comments, Ramdev has always maintained that he had no rift with Modi. 'I have known (Narendra) Modiji for fifteen years, and we have had some meetings before the 2014 elections. During those meetings, he told me that he supported my vision for a beautiful India by rooting out black money, not 100 per cent but 200 per cent. Because of my resolution to provide the country with a strong political alternative and as I came to realize that Modiji was that alternative, I put all my trust in him as has the rest of the country. We all hope and believe that he will prove to be the most successful prime minister the country has ever seen. You form an emotional attachment with some people in your lives, and that's what I have with Modiji. I don't represent any party and never will. Our friendship is based on a commonality of thought, principles, ideology and policies. And that would be the case with anyone, irrespective of his or her party,' he told *The Indian Express* in December 2016.[13]

His frustration with Modi was evident when he made a veiled attack on the Prime Minister during an interaction with journalists from *The Indian Express*. When he was asked about Indian army's surgical strike at terror camps in Pakistan occupied Kashmir, Ramdev subtly hinted that Modi had failed on two accounts—black money and poverty alleviation. 'Eliminating the evil is not violence. I think (Prime Minister Narendra) Modiji will also decimate Dawood Ibrahim, Masood Azhar and Hafiz Saeed, so that people of this country forget any grudges they have with him with regard to black money and poverty alleviation.'

When I asked him about his equation with the Prime Minister and the growing perception that the two have been drifting apart, he laughed uproariously. Then he composed himself and said: 'Why do you think I need any personal favour from Modi? I did not support him because I wanted something from him. He is the best we can have now. He is doing a good job. I'm a fakir and I don't want to meddle in the affairs of governance. Whenever I have raised any

---

[13]http://indianexpress.com/article/india/india-news-india/baba-ramdev-is-india-only-a-place-for-pak-artists-to-earn-crores-and-not-comment-on-terror-3727920/

issue, I have represented the public voice, not my personal demands. I could have interfered in the functioning of Modi government with my influence. I never did it. Even Prime Minister Modi asked me how I could withdraw so much.'

He may have claimed to have withdrawn from politics but he certainly plays an important role, and that's the reason why political leaders across party lines don't hesitate to offer him a red carpet. *Firstpost*'s Sandipan Sharma notes that many of these outlets in North India are Yadav-owned and they are an important vote bank in UP and Mewat, across Haryana, Rajasthan and Delhi. By helping them set up financially viable businesses, Ramdev has earned the loyalty of many movers and shakers in the Yadav group.[14]

It's the same reason why former UP Chief Minister Akhilesh Yadav has also tried to keep the Baba in good humour. He not only allotted 750 acres of land along the Yamuna Expressway but also laid the foundation of the food and herbal park in Greater Noida, alongside it.

❧

---

[14]http://www.firstpost.com/politics/after-cabinet-rank-ramdev-finds-a-political-home-in-bjps-warm-embrace-2195830.html

He Likes Demonetization, or Maybe Not

So when in November 2016, the Prime Minister announced his decision to ban the circulation of ₹500 and ₹1,000 currency notes, Ramdev was elated as it meant acknowledgement of his long-standing demand. He was quick to take credit. 'I had planted the seeds of demonetization. I continued the movement from 2009 to 2014 and asked the government to withdraw ₹500 and ₹1000 currency notes as it was the root cause of corruption, black money generation and terror and militant funding. Now with demonetization, black money generation, corruption and terror funding has stopped totally.'

While terming the demonetization drive as 'historic', he also listed out what he expected next from Modi. 'I am sure the Prime Minister would also rid black money from land dealings, gold, mining, politics and education. The Prime Minister fears none so he will also be able to bring back black money stashed abroad.'

But as days passed by, the Baba changed his mind. In an interview with *The Quint*, he said that corrupt bankers misled the Prime Minister and that demonetization will expose a ₹3–5 lakh crore scam in the economy. He also criticized the government for its decision to bring ₹2,000 currency notes—'Counterfeit ₹2,000 currency notes can come into the market and also encourage corruption as it is easy to store so it should not be printed.'

On 28 December 2016, he told newspersons: 'The results of the exercise, and whether the objectives have been fulfilled should be disclosed to the nation. The objectives are war on black money, ending corruption and bringing in economic transparency. *Ab notebandi ka daromadar taxmen ke upar hai jinka kaam January 1 se shuru hoga* (The onus is now on taxmen). They should not go after the poor, and not leave out the corrupt.'

He was just short of declaring that demonetization failed to achieve its goal—to put and end to black money in the country.

He also raised a finger of suspicion at RBI asking if almost all the demonetized ₹500 and ₹1,000 notes had been deposited in banks where was the black money. 'RBI officials have themselves engaged in corrupt practices since demonetization.' 'We have filed an RTI with the RBI,' he declared in a seminar in Lucknow. That was a major U-turn as immediately after Modi's 8 November declaration, Ramdev had claimed, as mentioned earlier, that demonetization would expose almost ₹4 lakh crore in black money.

He also hit out at a section in the banking sector, terming them as traitors. He was careful enough not to cause a political stir by sparing Modi from his attack but made no bones about his unhappiness over the way the entire demonetization drive was conducted. 'The intention of PM Narendra Modi vis-a-vis demonetization cannot be questioned. It is the implementation of the scheme, which has not been up to the mark. It could have been much better.' He alleged that some bank officials made a profit of ₹20 to ₹30 crores on every ₹100 crores that were being deposited and claimed that this was the main reason behind the cash crisis that the country went through during the demonetization drive. 'I have information that certain banks converted ₹100 to ₹200 crores of black money to white for some people in one go,' he said.

But in January, when the 50-day long demonetization drive was over, Ramdev softened his stance. In an interview with *The Asian Age*, he said: 'Demonetization is a big, brave and historic decision taken by the government. There are some initial problems, which are procedural in nature. It is a major step towards bringing economic transparency, reforms, responsibility and accountability in the country.'

His critics argue that his criticism of Modi's demonetization move stems from the fact that Patanjali's retail sales were hit hard by demonetization. As expected, Ramdev counters such criticism saying that he was well aware of its impact and it was he who had been demanding withdrawal of high value currencies for long.

'Yes, our business has suffered [in] some places, but [in]

some places it has surged too. Thirty per cent of Patanjali sales are through our own stores, which are equipped with card readers and digital payment systems. Here sales have risen 10 per cent in the wake of demonetization. Elsewhere they are down by 10 per cent. Volunteers of Bharat Swabhiman Trust helped lakhs of kirana store owners convert to digital payment methods,' he said.[15]

HOW BLACK IS MY ECONOMY

When Ramdev first raised the issue of black money, he started off by saying that ₹300 lakh crore of the total ₹400 lakh crore was stashed away in foreign banks. But his estimate seems to have changed currently. In a January 2017 interview to *The Asian Age*, he said: 'First of all, we must understand the economy of black money. Of the total black money, 85 per cent is internal against which the Union government has acted in a way of demonetization and 15 per cent is stashed away which is called cross-border black money.'

And he has offered his prescription to tackle the cross-border black money. 'The government must take three steps. First, the government must make declarations of names of ultimate beneficiaries or ownership of FDIs, as ₹20 lakh crore of black money brought in as FDI has come through Mauritius route under fake names. Secondly, the government must ensure a complete ban on uses of participatory or promissory note route and lastly by changing banking secrecy

---

[15]http://www.thehindubusinessline.com/opinion/columns/chitra-narayanan/patanjali-refined-oil/article9447996.ece

law which is helping foreign banks to easily siphon off black money from the country. Implementing these three steps will make way for action against cross-border black money.'

THE TAX REFORMER

Another bone of contention between Ramdev and the Modi government has been the government's slow progress on tax reforms. On 5 January 2014, at a function held at his ashram in Haridwar, which was attended by the then BJP prime ministerial candidate Narendra Modi, Ramdev declared his public support for Modi's candidature. In a press conference after the function, Ramdev told newspersons that an agreement was reached between him and Modi on various issues, including replacement of the present taxation system with a single transaction tax, elimination of corruption, steps to bring black money back from foreign banks, payment of a minimum income to farmers before the start of sowing, and primacy to Indian languages. In return of this agreement, the yoga guru had promised the party that he would send his followers to each home across the country to canvass support for the BJP.

Since 2010, Ramdev had been demanding abolition of all kinds of taxes and pitched for a single tax in the form of 'Banking Transaction Tax'. Much like the proposals by ArthaKranti, a Pune-based economic think-tank, Ramdev also wanted the government to do away with all Central and State taxes, barring customs duty, and demonetize big currency by withdrawing ₹500 and ₹1,000 notes from circulation. But unlike ArthaKranti, Ramdev believed that it was not practical to have only 1 or 2 per cent tax on banking transactions. Instead, he wanted 5 to 7 slabs for different categories such as manufacturing, trading, retailing, services, luxury, liquor and tobacco. His scheme would fetch the government ₹15 lakh crore to ₹30 lakh crore, Ramdev claimed. He had a solution for tax devolution as well. According to his plans, of total tax collections, 40 per cent each could go the Centre and the States, 18 per cent to local bodies and 2 per cent to banks. Ramdev claimed that the average tax burden would come down to 20–30 per cent from 60 per cent at present if his proposals were implemented, but it would not result in a revenue loss to the government. He wanted to keep labourers and farmers out of the tax net and recommended higher tax on sin goods like tobacco and liquor.

'We want simplification and automization of taxes. Political will is required for this. The BJP is willing to consider our proposal. We will make it a big issue in the forthcoming Lok Sabha elections (in 2014),' Ramdev had told the mediapersons, adding that he was also in touch with former BJP President Nitin Gadkari, who had come out with a similar tax idea. That is interesting as both Gadkari and Ramdev have vested interests.

At the function, Modi said: 'The present taxation system is a burden on common man. There is a need to reform it and introduce a new system. It is the need of the time.'

According to experts, under a transaction tax regime, evasion is technologically impossible because the bank will be responsible for the collection and payment of taxes, which will take place electronically. Such a tax is supposed to be simple—with little cost of collection, no filing of tax returns and no possibility of evasion. By implementing this proposal, it is argued that India can get rid of all the complicated taxes it has at present. There will, however, be no taxation of cash transactions because it will be difficult to implement. To ensure that people do not start transacting in cash alone, it was proposed that ₹500 and ₹1,000 currency notes should be demonetized.

Ramdev had suggested a three-phase implementation of the proposal. In the first phase, demonetization of big notes would happen to check black money and the process would not take more than six months. In the second phase, banks would strengthen their branch network so that more and more people had bank accounts, which would be the basis of most transactions. In the third phase, he proposed a voluntary disclosure of income scheme. The government might not have yet achieved success in introducing the Direct Taxes Code and the Goods & Services Tax (GST) after years of planning and discussions, but Ramdev is confident his proposal, which is 'better than GST', can be implemented within a year.

These words sound prophetic if one looks at Modi's decisions of last three years. Though not implemented in the same order as Ramdev had proposed, Modi has executed all three suggestions of the yoga guru. In the form of Jan-Dhan Yojana account, the Prime Minister launched a massive drive to bring the unbanked population under the banking system. He also declared a voluntary income disclosure scheme that came to an end in September 2016. And finally, in November 2016, he withdrew currencies of ₹500 and ₹1,000.

Obviously, Ramdev is happy to see his suggestions getting implemented, but he is in no mood to celebrate—'This is just the beginning. A lot needs to be done.'

Economists are, however, not excited about Ramdev's tax proposals for tax reforms. 'Commentators have highlighted that the international experience of transaction taxes shows that they do not support revenue collection of more than 2 per cent of the GDP, and even this declines over time. Most countries have given up on transaction taxes. Such taxes do not yield the 10 per cent of GDP that even a minimal government, such as the one that Modi is said to want to oversee, will need as revenue,' writes Ila Patnaik, professor at the National Institute of Public Finance and Policy, New Delhi.

❧

In Search of New Friends

Despite his explicit saffron tilt, the yoga guru has recently mended his relationship with rival political parties. The growing closeness between RJD chief Lalu Yadav and Ramdev is one such example. While Ramdev has been a supporter of Prime Minister Modi and the BJP, Lalu has been terming the BJP as communal for a long time and has constantly sided with the party pitted against it. Ramdev and Lalu have bitterly criticized each other in the past. In the run up to the Bihar Assembly elections, Lalu had called Ramdev 'mental' and Ramdev had called Lalu a 'beast'.

But the relationship has gone for a serious makeover in recent times. In May 2016, in front of a live camera, Ramdev gifted Patanjali products to the RJD chief and even applied cream on Lalu Yadav's face. Lalu also endorsed Ramdev's products saying: 'His products are in demand and he is doing good for the country. People are jealous of Baba Ramdev because he is highly successful.' Ramdev returned the compliment saying that some could not digest it as Laluji had stopped abusing him.

Again in December 2016, Ramdev met Lalu at his Patna home and taught him a few yoga postures, and then publicly praised him as a politician with huge importance for India's future. At Yadav's 10 Circular Road residence in Patna, which is allotted to his wife and former Bihar Chief Minister Rabri Devi, Ramdev joined the Yadav couple and their elder son Tej Pratap Yadav, Bihar's health minister. The RJD chief, who had not been keeping well, posted a photograph of this meeting on Twitter and tweeted: 'Baba Ramdev said: "You are a social and political heritage. Your keeping physically fit is necessary for the country's politics." I thank Baba for inquiring about my health.'

According to media reports, Ramdev is keen to get his niece married to Lalu Yadav's elder son, Tej Pratap Yadav. To boost production of his Patanjali products, Ramdev has even appointed Lalu's son-in-law as an agent or distributor of the same in Bihar.

Ramdev, however, rubbished such reports. 'I made Laluji practise pranayama, anulom-vilom and mandukasana exercises. I asked him to practise at least one asana daily. Considering this large nation's long future, it is necessary that he stay physically fit. He is a social and political heritage of the country.' Ramdev's nemesis Congress was quick to pick holes in Ramdev's praise for Lalu, whose RJD is in alliance with the grand old party in Bihar. 'Ramdev should first seek apology from Bihar's people for having earlier denigrated Yadav,' said a Congress leader.

Ramdev has also touched base with his former associates

in his battle against corruption—Delhi Chief Minister Kejriwal and Deputy Chief Minister Manish Sisodia. The duo were former members of India Against Corruption and later started a new political party, Aam Aadmi Party, which captured power in Delhi defeating Congress and BJP.

On 29 September 2016, Sisodia arrived at Patanjali Yogpeeth for a day's visit to seek cooperation and assistance of Patanjali Yogpeeth in training physical education teachers in yoga in government-run schools—as part of Delhi government's plan to make yoga, along with sports, mandatory in near future. He praised Ramdev saying that the yoga guru had changed the health scenario and left a mark on the corporate world with his expertise in yoga and Ayurveda and contribution to social causes. 'We want to make teachers and students yoga perfect and this will change the health scenario in Delhi. Yoga is an ancient Indian practice, which Ramdev has redefined. It's an honour to be here and have assistance from the yoga guru in making Delhi and our country a better place to live in,' said Sisodia.

Ramdev assured Sisodia of the same cooperation as he was offering in yoga training at Haryana government schools and to Border Security Force personnel. Ramdev praised the Delhi government for its initiative of teaching yoga in government schools. He said lakhs of students enrolled in Delhi schools would benefit from this initiative and Patanjali Yogpeeth would commit the maximum number of yoga teachers and training sessions.

It may have sounded like a businesslike meeting, but the political undercurrent was evident. Kejriwal's Delhi government has been at loggerheads with Modi's Union government. In fact, Kejriwal and Sisodia have been two of the harshest critics of Modi, who has Ramdev as one of his strongest supporters. But when reporters probed the yoga guru about this new and revived friendship, he refused to take side: 'Modi is doing a good job and so is Delhi Chief Minister Arvind Kejriwal and his deputy, Manish Sisodia. We are saints and hence we welcome anyone coming to us for a good cause. We don't consider political affiliations or religion, sect or community angle. For good causes, saints welcome everyone with full heart and blessings.'

If this was not enough to fuel speculation that all was not well between Modi and Ramdev, his sudden praise of Mamata Banerjee came as a rude shocker. In December 2016, when West Bengal Chief Minister Mamata Banerjee had launched a scathing attack on Modi over the issue of demonetization, Ramdev lauded her saying that she had enough credential to become the prime minister. 'There should not be any question regarding her credibility in politics. If son of a chai-wala could become prime minister, Mamataji could also become prime minister,' Ramdev told reporters.[16]

'In politics, Mamataji is the symbol of honesty and simplicity. I love her simplicity. She wears chappals and ordinary saris. I believe she does not have black money,' he said.

---

[16]http://indiatoday.intoday.in/story/prime-minister-narendra-modi-mamata-banerjee-chai-wala-baba-ramdev-demonetisation-black-money/1/826355.html

He even tried to take credit for her rise in the state. 'Once during my visit to West Bengal, when Left Front was in power, I had said the Leftists should go and Mamataji should come to power. And exactly it happened thereafter.'

But this appreciation could be spurred by business interests as Ramdev is hoping to set up Patanjali units in West Bengal. That's the reason he sought to defend Mamata's opposition to demonetization, which he had initially supported with great vigour. 'I think she is not opposed to the demonetization move per se. But I feel she is not happy the way it was implemented,' Ramdev said on the sidelines of a seminar.

❧

RSS Remains the Final Frontier

The one thing that worries the yoga guru most is the fact that he has not been able to win complete trust and support of the RSS. The RSS has supported him in his business ventures but he has faced resistance from the organization when it comes to his moves in education and politics. It was responsible for Modi government's reluctance to recognize the Vedic education board proposed by Ramdev.

In an article titled 'Bazaar mein brand Bharat ka danka' in a recent edition of RSS mouthpiece *Panchjanya*, Ramdev was generously praised for his 'Made in India' products which gave a tough competition to other multinational companies.[17]

'Swadeshi ko badava dene mein sabse ahem bhumika yog guru swami Ramdev ki rahi hai. Patanjali ne bazaar mein aata noodles utar kar naami kampaniyo ka karobar seemit kar diya. Aaj Patanjali dwara nirmit swadeshi khadya vastuyo

---

[17]http://www.deccanchronicle.com/160106/nation-current-affairs/article/rss-hails-ramdev-products

ki mang badd chuki hai. (Ramdev has played a vital role in promoting indigenous products. Introduction of Patanjali's aata noodles has led to the limiting of the business of these multinational companies. Today, the demand of these Made in India products have gone up immensely).'

The article came at a time when Patanjali was facing trouble with Food Safety and Standards Authority of India (FSSAI), which had said that Patanjali's instant noodles had not obtained mandatory product approvals from it. According to the FSSAI, the license issued to Patanjali Ayurved Ltd and Patanjali Food and Herbal Park was for manufacturing a range of products but that was exclusive of noodles.

Unlike RSS, Ramdev has avoided championing the cause of Hindutva, but he has subtly supported many RSS agendas. Though Ramdev has refrained from giving any religious discourse, he has never shied away from wearing his Hindu pride on his sleeve. Speaking at the inauguration of the 8th Hindu Spiritual and Service Fair 2016, he said that Christians did charity but also indulged in conversions, while Hindus refrained from such practice. He is well aware that such statements are music to the ears of RSS brass as they have been campaigning against religious conversions. 'They do service—run schools, colleges and hospitals, and with that they also convert. We do service, including teaching yoga free of cost. But we have not changed anybody's religion but only their lives.' He said people are often told to learn charity from Christians but lakhs of Hindu sadhus and charitable trusts are also offering such services.

According to *Gurus: Stories of India's Leading Babas*, a book by veteran journalist Bhavdeep Kang, Ramdev had proposed a plan to revive the BJP in 2010, offering to merge his Bharat Swabhiman Andolan with it and jointly campaign for political and social change. But RSS rejected this plan. Ramdev had suggested setting up an 11-member panel to restructure the BJP constitution. He had also mooted constituting a 6-member committee, comprising two nominees each from the RSS, BJP and the Bharat Swabhiman Andolan, with senior BJP leader L.K. Advani to oversee the revival plan. The plan was discussed by RSS brass at its Udupi meet in March 2011. 'A few weeks later, on 7 April 2011, RSS Sarsanghchalak Mohan Rao Bhagwat attended a function organized by Ramdev in Haridwar. After it was over, the two met in private and Bhagwat handed over a written note to Baba Ramdev suggesting he speak to the BJP directly. In effect, the RSS had rejected his proposal.'

When I asked Ramdev about this episode, he laughed it off. 'That's why I'm going to write my autobiography. People are writing too many things depending on hearsay.' Not surprising then that when detractors suggested that Ramdev's Ramlila Maidan agitation was backed by the RSS, he was desperate to distance himself from the organization. 'Representatives of all religions and social action groups were there to support the movement. How can you simply say that it was an RSS event?' he said.

Haryana: Ramdev's New Breeding Ground

On 4 June 2011, when Ramdev launched his fast against corruption at Delhi's Ramlila Maidan, he kept asking his followers from different states to give a shout-out. How many people from Assam? How many from Uttarakhand? How many from Maharashtra? They made noise but not like those from Haryana. When he shouted out Haryana, the roar was deafening. 'Looks like all of Haryana has packed their bags and landed here,' he said.

Certainly, it makes sense for the Haryana government to make the best use of his popularity in his home state. The BJP government in the state has appointed Ramdev as the state's brand ambassador. Also Chief Minister Khattar, who owes his elevation to the top post in the state to Prime Minister Modi, a yoga aficionado, wants to promote yoga and Ayurveda in a big way. Ramdev as the brand ambassador perfectly matched the portfolio. In typical Ramdev lingo, the yoga guru declared: 'The day is not far off when Haryana will become India's first yogic state.' Later, the State government offered him a cabinet rank though Ramdev refused the status saying he was a 'fakir' and he was above respect and disrespect. 'I don't need any rank to promote yoga,' he said.

But he has been true to his job, often making valiant attempts to save Haryana's image. The brand ambassador of the state was at work, when he sought to brush off the violent Jat protests there in February 2016, that brought Haryana to standstill for days, as mere aberrations: 'Haryana is both progressive and aggressive. But what we need is to balance between the two to prosper. The unfortunate episode was an exception, violent protests is not the real culture and tradition of Haryana.'

Ironically, Ramdev supported Jat reservation but appealed to the protestors to run the movement peacefully. 'There is a need for a national policy on reservation so that no caste feels oppressed. It is unfortunate that Jat reservation movement has turned violent causing loss of lives and properties. Violence is not the solution to any problem. I belong to Haryana, so I understand the sentiments of people of my home,' said Ramdev. It's not surprising to see Ramdev comment on reservations as he himself claims to have faced caste discrimination. 'This discrimination prevails even among sadhus. Many sadhus in India don't want to recognize me as one of them because I'm not a Brahmin,' he told me in May 2016.

It's not Chief Minister Khattar only, Haryana's Health Minister Anil Vij has also been rather upfront about his support to Ramdev. 'Ramdev is on a mission to make India into Bharat with his company making indigenous products [which are] worth ₹10,000 crore today. I wish to see his company grow to lakhs of crores so that foreign companies which take money to foreign land could be thrown away,' Vij has said this on record. He has even announced a donation of ₹21 lakh to Ramdev's Acharyakulam in Bhiwani.

Vij has also often talked about his plans to impart yoga training in schools so that it reaches every doorstep. Physical education teachers and Anganwadi workers will be trained at Patanjali Yogpeeth in Haridwar so that they can teach yoga to small children. The Khattar government has decided to open 6,500 vyamshalas in almost all villages in Haryana and trainers would be engaged for children, youth and senior citizens. An AYUSH wing was being established in all the hospitals of Haryana for which 550 doctors would have to do a refresher course under the supervision of the yoga guru.

Following this, a meeting held at Patanjali Yogpeeth on 14 May 2016, which was chaired by Baba Ramdev and the Haryana State Council of Educational Research and Training, has recommended that Sanskrit should be made compulsory in all schools under the state board from Class VI to XII. According to the minutes of the meeting, the participants recommended that 'Sanskrit Vigyan' should include the study of the Vedas, Upanishads, Bhagwad Gita, yoga, Ayurveda, literature and grammar. It was also proposed that yoga should be included in Hindi textbooks from Class I to V.

Haryana government has signed a Memorandum of Understanding (MoU) with Ramdev's Patanjali Yogpeeth for the development of 'world's largest herbal forest' at Morni in Panchkula district where 'species of all medicinal plants would be made available'. 'This herbal forest, which would be completely developed in the coming 2–3 years, would put Haryana on the international map. It would not only provide a platform to the researchers from [all over the] world but also emerge as an international tourist destination,' Vij said. The Central government has also assured its full assistance to develop the forest.

In his eagerness to please Ramdev, in 2016, Haryana Chief Secretary Deepinder Singh Dhesi had issued a directive asking top bureaucrats to turn up at a 2-hour training session, starting at 5 a.m., with the state brand ambassador and yoga guru. The session was held a week before the International Yoga Day celebrations in Chandigarh on 21 June, which was attended by Prime Minister Narendra Modi. Despite directions from Dhesi, only 5 out of the total 21 additional chief secretaries turned up while all others, including the 15 principal secretaries, gave the event a miss.

Of course, Haryana government's decision to appoint Ramdev as brand ambassador had its share of criticism. Slamming the appointment, the Congress questioned the yoga guru's educational qualifications. Former Haryana Finance Minister Sampat Singh sought a rollback of the decision saying that those people who were already teaching yoga and practising Ayurveda in the state were highly qualified and held doctorate degrees. 'Ayurvedic doctors have MS and MD degrees. Ramdev's appointment is like a joke. The government should give preference to qualified doctors and trainers,' said the Congress leader.

Singh did not even spare the chief minister for the decision to rename the gurukuls in the state as archaryakulam. 'It is ridiculous as both the words mean the same. The government should have promoted and upgraded the existing 35 gurukuls instead of renaming them,' said Singh.

❧

The Educationist and Reformer

If yoga and Ayurveda have helped Ramdev create his business empire and brand equity, the yoga guru wants to leverage this fame to bring back traditional education in India. Inside Patanjali Yogpeeth, he has already set up a university, an Ayurveda college, an acharyakulam school and two gurukuls. The university website states it is '...a manifestation of divine vision of His Holiness Swami Ramdev and Honorable Acharya Balkrishna to establish **An Integral Center of Education Excellence** blending all spectrums of oriental wisdom and scientific knowledge.'

But this seems to be the first phase of a grand expansion plan, which includes revolutionizing the education system with a perfect mix of ancient Indian wisdom and values with modern science. Ramdev plans to to start a world-class university in India in the next five years to educate around 1 lakh students in different streams. He had said during his address on 'Yoga and Inner Peace' at an event in Houston, US, on 23 August that the standard of education in his university would be at par with Ivy League. 'This university will be as reputed as the ancient higher-learning institutions—Nalanda and Takshashila—so that students from all around the world would opt for India for higher education.' The proposed university will focus on three major areas—health, business and education—and will come up in Greater Noida. The UP government has already allotted 25 acres of land for the university.

In an interview to *The Economic Times*, Ramdev said that the university would produce future Olympians for India. 'We are coming up with the world's largest university in National Capital region, where 80 per cent of earnings of Patanjali will be spent on education and sports,' he said. The cost of the project would be around ₹25,000 crore. At another function at Vatsalya Gram Centre in Vrindavan, he said: 'The standard of education would be such that students of Harvard and Cambridge would be tempted to study here.'

Ramdev has also indicated plans to set up a university in Haryana. Interestingly, he made the announcement on the same day the BJP government in Haryana had announced its decision to set up an AYUSH University at Kurukshetra. In fact, the existing Shri Krishna Government Ayurvedic College, Kurukshetra, will be upgraded to a university. 'The government will set up this university (at Kurukshetra), but we (under Patanjali) too will set up one. A resolution to this effect will be passed in Haryana Assembly soon,' he told reporters in a press conference where Haryana Chief Minister Manohar Lal Khattar was also present. He was too eager to clarify that Patanjali Yogpeeth would not seek or take any financial help from Haryana government. 'We will seek legal advice from the government.' Later, speaking at Happening Haryana event, Ramdev had announced his plan to invest ₹5,000 crore to set up a university and an international health centre in the state.

Khattar also said that in his capacity as brand ambassador of Haryana, Ramdev would play a guiding role in setting up the AYUSH University at Kurukshetra, which would have the facility of in-patient and out-patient departments, pharmacy and a herbal garden.

It's not just about university education only. Ramdev has a much bigger dream—to take his 'traditional value-based education' to every nook and corner of the country. Currently, he runs an acharyakulam school in Haridwar which is affiliated to the CBSE board but has special focus on the Hindu philosophy, the Shastras, Sanskrit and the Vedas. He wants to set up 1,000 such acharyakulams across the country. Modelled after the gurukul pattern of education, Ramdev calls these schools 'a fusion of modern and Vedic education'. The main aim of an acharyakulam is to prepare proven scholars in grammar, philosophy, the Upanishads, Vedas, Vedic literature, Vedic mathematics, Indian history and Raj Dharma. It also aspires to prepare students with the power to give social, spiritual, economic, scientific and political leadership. In short, it intends to groom leaders for a modern India.

'With modern education, we will link ancient science. The youths graduating from the school will behave like rishis (sages). Acharyakulam will be a unique school that will train both the students and their parents.' During one of my interactions with him at Haridwar, I could sense that Ramdev places a lot of emphasis on the education of parents. He believes that parents are the most influential teachers for children and how they behave at home imapcts the child's personality. 'An ideal student can be produced when he has an ideal home,' he says.

The schools will be of two types—fully residential and day boarding from classes I to XII. Patanjali is actively seeking land and donors to set up these acharyakulams. The yoga guru wants a self-sustaining model with schools operating on a non-profit basis. Patanjali Yogpeeth is promising that the names of donors will be displayed on the front gate of the school, letter pad, building and school vehicles. The minimum land required for residential units has been fixed at 10 acres while 2 to 5 acres is needed for day boarding. Moreover, each person interested in setting up such a school has been asked to find another 50–100 donors.

The second big residential acharyakulam is coming up in Haryana. The State government has allotted 10 acres of land and Patanjali is investing ₹25 crore in setting up the school, which will have the capacity to accommodate about 2,500 students. Clearly, Haryana is going to be a major hub of all educational endeavours of Ramdev.

But he is not happy to keep his brand of school affiliated to CBSE and plans to run an autonomous education board. Ramdev runs a Haridwar-based Vedic Education Research Institute, which had proposed a Vedic Education Board

(VEB) for the country in early 2016. The proposal made in March 2016 detailed how VEB would contribute to the Indian education system by providing a blend of human education of Aurobindo, archaistic education of Maharshi Dayanand and Vedanta education of Swami Vivekananda. 'Unfortunately, no effort has been made to make the education system purely Indian, swadeshi, purifying it or making it fully scientific,' writes Balkrishna in an editorial in *Yog Sandesh* magazine, published by Patanjali Yogpeeth.

VEB proposes to formulate the curriculum, prepare textbooks and conduct examinations. The proposed board also sought to frame guidelines for recruitment of teachers in its affiliated schools. This was equivalent to creation of a parallel institute to National Council for Teacher Education (NCTE), which regulates teacher education and recruitment in the country. If permitted, it will allow them to sustain their model of education up to Class XII, which the CBSE currently does not permit.

But Ramdev's proposal was dismissed by the then school education secretary S.C. Khuntia, who had serious reservations about the government recognizing a private school board. Khuntia red-flagged the proposal at a meeting chaired by Prime Minister Narendra Modi on the ground that the state's sanction for a private board would open the doors for similar requests from other unrecognized school boards. No private board is currently recognized by the Union government.

The meeting was called by the Prime Minister to seek HRD Ministry's position on the proposal submitted by

Ramdev. As an alternative to Ramdev's plan, the HRD Ministry suggested that the government empower Maharshi Sandipani Rashtriya Ved Vidya Pratisthan (MSRVVP) in Ujjain to conduct exams in Vedic and Sanskrit education and recognize Vedic pathshalas and Sanskrit medium schools. MSRVVP is a fully-funded autonomous body under the HRD ministry, which runs programmes to promote the oral tradition of the Vedas.

However, the primary objection to Ramdev's board came from RSS Joint General Secretary Krishna Gopal, who reportedly influenced the then HRD Minister Smriti Irani to take a stand against Vedic Education Board. Reviving traditional Indian education has been a pet project of RSS too, and the organization did not want Ramdev to fly away with all the glory. His brand of schools may come in direct competition with Vidya Bharati Schools run by the RSS. Ramdev was hopeful that Prime Minister Narendra Modi would overrule Irani and her subsequent removal from the ministry kindled his hope of getting an approval. In my meeting with Ramdev in May 2016, he had told me that the approval would come in just a couple of months. 'Wait, the top leader is yet to take a decision.'

He is still waiting and, if insiders are to be believed, the yoga guru is certainly not amused with Modi's reluctance to give a go ahead. He is also not happy with Modi government's attitude towards Vedic learning. Speaking at an international conference on the Vedas, he made a scathing attack on the Union government and asked the Narendra Modi government to 'loosen its purse strings' for promoting the Vedas as has been done for minority institutions and proposed setting up a centre for Vedic learning. 'The government has given money to madrassas. It is a good thing. We are not criticizing anybody. We do not disrespect any other faith and it is not our intention to belittle anyone. The Modi government talks of "Sabka Saath Sabka Vikas" (equal growth for all), but don't our Vedas come under that?' he asked.

'The organisers of this conference have invested several hundred crores of rupees on this event. But our government does not have money to spend on Vedas. I think, given the importance of this ancient wisdom of our country, they (Centre) should have poured in several thousands of crores of rupees on it. Now, they are spending on Sanskrit also. But, for Vedas, there is no money,' Ramdev said. He also pitched for establishing a Vedic temple-cum-university that would serve not just as a mere worship place but also as a knowledge centre for propagation of Vedic teachings. 'Even UNESCO has acknowledged the importance of Vedas and called Vedic chants as a cultural heritage, and it was time our own government gave it its due too. It is my hope that like for yoga, the Modi government would also do the needful to promote Vedas,' he said.[18]

According to Ramdev, there is a gap in the understanding between the Vedic scholars and modern scientists. 'Our aim and mission is to create a confluence of ancient science and modern science. People who know Vedic science are

---

[18]http://www.dnaindia.com/india/report-government-not-spending-money-for-promotion-of-vedas-baba-ramdev-2063220

not aware of quantum physics, space science, chemistry and other contemporary areas, and many of the modern scientists do not have idea about the Vedic science. We want both of them to interact with each other and we will plan a meet of top scientists and renowned Vedic scholars soon for that.'

He believes that Vedas can offer solutions to modern world aberrations such as communal discordance, war-mongering and consumerism. 'We should endeavour to build a Vedic India and ultimately a Vedic world for benefit of all mankind. We want modernity with spirituality,' he said.

Ramdev's influence in the education sector doesn't end with his own brand of schools and universities. A government appointed high-powered committee headed by H.R. Nagendra, who is apparently Prime Minister Modi's yoga guru as well, made various recommendations regarding the setting up of yoga departments in universities. The committee also recommended that knowledge of Baba Ramdev's Patanjali Yogpeeth, S-VYASA Yoga University headed by Nagendra and some other institutes could be used for setting up of these departments.

The central universities have been directed to include modules of yoga teaching and training in both the graduate and undergraduate courses in physiotherapy by the University Grants Commission (UGC). As desired by Modi, the Central government wants the universities to explore the likelihood of a giving preference to candidates who have a certain level of expertise in yoga for admission to a Bachelor's course in physiotherapy. The committee headed by Nagendra recommended the yoga syllabi for a 4-year Bachelor's course and a 2-year Master's course in physiotherapy.

❧

Land Controversies

Ramdev may have lofty goals but his project in Nepal landed in a controversy after a media report claimed that Patanjali Ayurved group invested more than ₹150 crore in the country without official approval. The Foreign Investment and Technology Transfer Act requires any foreign investor to get permission from the Investment Board Nepal or the Department of Industries before investing in Nepal. The report in Nepal's largest selling newspaper *Kantipur Daily* said Ramdev failed to seek such mandatory permissions.

Ramdev denied the allegations in a statement released on 28 November, saying his company did not flout any local law. The proposed investment from Patanjali Ayurved Limited will flow into Nepal only after completing all due legal processes. According to Ramdev, Patanjali Yogpeeth of Nepal, which is likely to be Ramdev's partner in the country, did not receive any sort of investment from India. Nepali businessman Upendra Mahato and his wife Dr Samata Prasad own Patanjali Yogpeeth Pvt Ltd. Patanjali has been exploring the possibility of 'herbal farming' as well as buying rare herbs for his Ayurveda plants from Nepal, in collaboration with Mahato's company.

'Entire investment in Patanjali Yogpeeth in Nepal has come from Mahato and his wife. When we invest in the company in future, which we plan to do, we will follow the prevalent laws of Nepal and take approval from the concerned government authorities,' Ramdev said in the statement. He doesn't forget to mention that that proceeds from that company will not be distributed to the investor but 'will be spent on philanthropic activities'.

Ironically, just five days before this statement, Ramdev himself had announced in a press meet that Patanjali had invested ₹150 crores in an Ayurvedic factory in Nepal and was planning to further invest ₹500 crore in the future. He claimed his investment was meant for the production of organic medicine and other items, which would generate 20,000 jobs in the country. The next day, Nepal's President Bidya Devi Bhandari inaugurated the Patanjali factory in southern Nepal's Bara district. Prime Minister Pushpa Kamal Dahal and Minister for Agriculture Gauri Shankar Chaudhary were also present on the occasion.

And this was not the only controversy he generated in the neighbouring country. Ramdev's bid to get nearly 134-hectare land for an Ayurveda college-cum-hospital in western Nepal's Dang district also ran into rough weather. Nepal Sanskrit University in Dang, apparently had agreed to lease out to Patanjali Yogpeeth a vast stretch of the land under its possession for forty years, but before the deal was signed, a section of the university administration opposed the move saying university land could not be leased out to anyone for more than ten years. Ramdev plans to build an Ayurvedic hospital, an ashram, a herb garden and a cowshed on the land.

In February 2016, Himachal Pradesh government cancelled 28 acres of land allotted to Patanjali Yogpeeth Trust on lease at Sadhupul in Solan district citing irregularities. In 2010, the BJP government had given the land to Patanjali Yogpeeth for a payment of ₹17 lakh and a 99-year lease at a token annual fee of Re 1. 'It's a political conspiracy. We have followed the legal procedure,' sais Balkrishna.

In 2009, an NRI couple gifted Ramdev a 900-acre island in Scotland called Peace Island. The Enforcement Directorate under UPA government filed a case against Ramdev, investigating a possible violation of the Foreign Exchange Management Act for this. The directorate closed this case after BJP came to power. Another money laundering case pending against Balkrishna was closed in October 2014. Two months later, the CBI filed a closure report to the case of the mysterious disappearance of Ramdev's guru Shankar Dev in 2007 from the Patanjali Yogpeeth campus.

In 2011, the CBI filed a case against Balkrishna on charge of holding a passport made on forged documents. His high school degree—'Purv Madhyma' and Sanskrit degree—'Shastri' from Sampurna Nand Sanskrit University—do not allegedly exist on records. Congress leader Digvijay Singh accused Balkrishna of committing crime in Nepal and fleeing to India, a charge later denied by the Nepal government.

Balkrishna disappeared in 2012 after CBI summoned him in the forgery case and the Enforcement Directorate later registered a case against him under the Prevention of Money Laundering Act for alleged illegal remittances. Balkrishna was imprisoned for a month on charges of carrying a false passport—the government said he was a Nepali passing himself off as an Indian. Balkrishna recalled a phase when, out of fear that the government might plant drugs in the factories, he hired sniffer dogs to scout not only the premises but also employees' lunch boxes to ensure no one was attempting sabotage. The cases were dropped after the National Democratic Alliance (NDA) came to power in 2014. The two-year CBI investigation against him found 'no evidence' of wrongdoing and he was given a clean chit.

In 2013, the Uttarakhand government registered 96 cases against the Patanjali Yogpeeth and its sister concerns in Haridwar for violation of the Zamindari Abolition and Land Reforms (ZALR) Act and the Indian Stamps Act. The then Chief Minister Vijay Bahuguna had said that several of the properties held by the Patanjali trust had turned out to be benami transactions with no trace of the owners. The cases under the ZALR Act included encroachment upon about 7.8 acres of gram sabha and government land by the Trust in villages Shantarshah and Aurangabad. The Trust had purchased 387.5 acres of land in villages Aurangabad and Shivdaspur for establishing the Patanjali University. The varsity was built on about 20 acres and the rest was being used for agriculture and possibly being retained as a land bank for future commercial uses. The Trust purchased 84.86

acres of land in village Mustafabad in the name of Patanjali Food and Herbal Park without seeking necessary permission from the authorities. 'This was a serious violation of the law and suitable action would be taken against the Trust,' said Bahuguna.

Similarly, the permission granted to purchase 141.17 acres of land for manufacturing Ayurvedic medicines in village Mustafabad was being violated by using the land for manufacturing, warehousing and marketing of a whole range of Patanjali products like flour, oil, juices, honey, soaps, toothpaste and shampoo.

The former Chief Minister also alleged that there had been 63 cases of undervaluation of the stamp duty that caused a loss of ₹10 crores to the State exchequer. Later, the Uttarakhand government registerd 11 more cases of stamp duty evasion against Ramdev's Patanjali Yogpeeth Trust.

A petition was filed before the Indore bench of Madhya Pradesh High Court, challenging the allotment of 40 acres land to Patanjali Ayurved in Pithampur industrial area in Dhar district to set up a food-processing unit. The business bench of the High Court, comprising of Justice P.K. Jaiswal and Justice Virendra Singh has sought an explanation from Shivraj Singh Chouhan's government over the allotment of land to the company by Audyogik Kendra Vikas Nigam (AKVN).

According to petitioner Anand Mohan Mathur, who is a senior advocate, the State government floated no tender for allocating land worth several crores. Apart from the allocation of the land, the government also obliged Ramdev by giving assurance that his product would be sold through ration shops and cooperative societies. Advocate Mathur said that the government should have been transparent and a clean procedure for the allocation of land should have been followed.

Maharashtra Congress MLA Sharad Ranpise has alleged that the Maharashtra government has incurred a loss of ₹209 crore by giving land at a concessional rate to Patanjali's food processing unit in Mihan in Nagpur. According Ranpise, Mihan SEZ project was being allotted at the rate of ₹1.16 crore per acre and, by this rate Patanjali should have got its share of 230 acre at the cost of ₹267 crore. Instead, the government charged only ₹58.65 crore from Patanjali, which means that the land was allotted at the rate of ₹25.5 lakh per acre. Countering the allegation, Minister of State Madan Yerawar said that since the land that was given to Patanjali is outside the Mihan SEZ and is underdeveloped so its cost is less.

Ramdev denies that the government offered any special favour to him. 'We got 230 acres of land from the Maharashtra government for food park through an open tender. I even invited other people to join, at half the rate, but nobody came forward. I think that's what the government and Modiji should do now—offer land to Indian enterprises with some subsidies, so that India becomes world's largest manufacturing hub,' he said.

❧

BEND IT LIKE BABA

The Swadeshi Warrior

With all the aggressive investments in food parks, mega shelters for cows, Ayurveda research, swadeshi jeans and integrating farmers to the markets, Baba Ramdev aims to end the hegemony of international companies on the Indian economy.

As brand ambassador for Patanjali, Ramdev has urged his followers to show their patriotism by buying products only made by companies that are fully Indian-owned. Goods made in India by foreign companies don't qualify. 'Why should these companies take the profits out of the country,' he says.

'When we want Indians winning medals in sports, why can't we develop the same spirit in economic pursuits and excel in businesses on our own? My fight is against foreign companies trying to take over our economy,' says Ramdev.

And his battle is not restricted to sports only. India may have made its name in global landscape as an IT giant, but that's not enough for Ramdev. 'My dream is that somebody in India sets up a parallel network to Google. God willing, one day we'll set up our own Facebook and Google. And Gandhiji used to say about swadeshi, that what is available in your country, use that first, what is not there, seek help from outside. So the principle of swadeshi is scientific and not a compromise,' he had said in a newspaper interview.

In his advertisements, Ramdev gives a new spin to the very idea of economic freedom. He appeals to the buyers to bring economic independence to India by buying Patanjali products because they are 'home-made, original and unadulterated'.

One of the advertisements even quoted freedom fighter Ramprasad Bismil, to motivate buyers to severe India's dependence from the 'profit sucking' multinational companies—they are the clones of the original culprit East India Company—and make India great again. 'India got political independence from East India Company, now it's time to get economic independence,' says Ramdev.

Critics have slammed Ramdev for his 'ridiculous' idea of economic independence. 'Having willingly embraced the economic reforms in 1991, the floodgates were opened precisely for sustaining the economic freedom which Baba Ramdev is alluding to. The difference being, his idea of a pro-business world was an evanescent period in the 1980s whose logical culmination was the pro-private tilt toward the end of the same decade. What Baba Ramdev's philosophy does is it even makes a case for a return to that period, one that is now widely critiqued as a "crisis of governability",' writes columnist Suraj Kumar Thube in *DailyO*.[19]

And at a time when Prime Minister Narendra Modi is travelling to far corners of the world seeking foreign direct investment, Ramdev's swadeshi slogan raises a pitch contradicting Modi's dream of making India the hub of manufacturing. Modi has been busy wooing foreign investors to set up factories in India while Ramdev's declared goal is to drive them out.

PM Modi's efforts are seemingly paying dividends. A recent UNCTAD study estimated that FDI into India could touch $60 billion in 2016, up from $44 billion in 2015. The 2015 FDI flow was itself 28 per cent higher than the previous year. But Ramdev sees no dichotomy between what Modi has been trying to achieve and what he has been preaching, 'I have no problem with FDI in sectors where India is not self-reliant.'

There could be some history lessons for Ramdev in India's earlier attempts to drive out MNCs and public reaction to swadeshi brands. A cover story on Ramdev in *Open* magazine makes some interesting observations:[20]

It was after Emergency of the mid-1970s that the Socialist leader George Fernandes went after MNCs, directing his attack mainly at Coca-Cola, the American soft drink that sold a lifestyle with every glug. In

---

[19]http://www.dailyo.in/politics/patanjali-baba-ramdev-economic-freedom-swadeshi/story/1/12386.html

[20]http://www.openthemagazine.com/article/cover-story/baba-ramdev-the-karma-yogi

1977, with the Janata regime in power, the company was forced out of the Indian market. But Fernandes failed to provide an alternative business model. Double Seven, a brand backed by him—launched by the then Prime Minister Morarji Desai—was supposed to fill the vacuum, but it proved a no match for the 'real thing'. The opposition to MNCs was stronger in those days. It was a time when university campuses from Delhi to Kerala were valorising Chilean leader Salvador Allende and erupting in anti-MNC slogans. Such a groundswell of sentiment should have helped Double Seven succeed. But it lacked the fizz, so to speak. Later, Ramesh Chauhan's Thums Up did establish itself as India's top cola, but was just another cola and didn't make an overt swadeshi pitch, focusing instead on youthful verve and fun.

Three reasons can be ascribed to the failure of the anti-MNC struggle of the late 70s. One, Fernandes and Modern Foods failed to address the consumer's need for world-class products. Two, the desi challenge to Western cultural domination was not as robust as it is today. And three, the flaws of the Nehruvian economic model had not yet been fully exposed.

Market analysts argue that ideological fervour alone is not enough to sustain local brands and business models. They require either unique products or those that meet needs in differentiated ways. One major reason that Patanjali is better placed to make a go of a swadeshi pitch against MNCs is that it offers functional benefits packed with an emotional appeal. 'It works' or 'Good stuff at a good price' is more likely to be heard of a Patanjali product than 'We are opposed to MNCs and their cultural messages'.

A Nielsen Global Brand Origin Survey released in April 2016 also brings some cheers to Patanjali. According to the survey, almost 75 per cent of global respondents, on average, say that a brand's country of origin is as important as or more important than other criteria such as price and quality.[21]

The findings were based on responses from more than 30,000 online respondents in 61 countries spanning 40 categories. According to Nielsen, the main factors for consumers choosing local over global brands are better value for money (50 per cent), national pride (37 per cent), positive previous experience (27 per cent), sale or promotional prices (27 per cent), safer ingredients or processing (26 per cent), and organic or all-natural options (22 per cent). Nearly 60 per cent say they buy local brands to support local businesses. Developing-market respondents are more likely to say that local brands are more attuned to their personal likes. Interestingly, national pride takes precedence over price or quality as a purchasing criterion in Asia Pacific, Africa and the Middle East. It is the only selection factor for which there is a notable difference between local and global brands.

---

[21]http://www.nielsen.com/in/en/press-room/2016/nielsen-75-percent-of-global-consumers-list-brand-origin-as-key-purchase-driver.html

In Southeast Asia, 52 per cent said they preferred to purchase local brands over large global brands. Even though consumers in developing markets view global brands positively for quality and innovation, the prevailing outlook is that their costs are still high. Seventy-two per cent of respondents in Asia Pacific say global brands are more expensive than local brands, while the sentiment that local brands have a better understanding of consumers' needs and preferences is also highest in developing markets.

The popularity of ayurvedic and traditional herbal ingredients in modern consumer products in India coincides with a resurgence of Hindu nationalism.

'One of the ways in which Hindu nationalism maintains itself is by highlighting its own uniqueness and antiquity. The search for objects and practices of national antiquity, which isn't peculiar to India, has been seamlessly merged with contemporary consumerism. People like Baba Ramdev and Shri Shri Ravi Shankar have capitalized on these dual desires by claiming to package "tradition" as a product of modern convenience. Their own status within Indian society offers legitimacy to what they claim is tradition,' says Meera Ashar, deputy director of the South Asia Research Institute at the Australian National University in Canberra.[22]

❦

---

[22]https://www.bloomberg.com/news/articles/2016-11-30/yoga-gurus-the-leaders-behind-india-s-hottest-consumer-products

The Social Media Guru

There is no doubt that Ramdev has attained a cult following through his yoga discourse, but complacency is not a word in his dictionary. He may he have harped on the benefits of ancient Indian wisdom, but he never hesitates to accept and utilize modern forms and tools of communication. The saffron-clad yoga guru is a big exponent of social media.

With nearly 7 lakh followers on Twitter, around 80 lakh likes on his Facebook page and an active presence on Instagram and Pinterest, the gregarious Ramdev, who rarely says no to photographs or a selfie, knows the importance of constantly 'being in the mind space' of his followers. Often, his team belts out social media tutorials in his yoga camps. Before he takes stage, people are told about the benefits of social media and how these communication tools can be used to gather facts and avoid rumours. The team appeals to people to connect directly with the guru through various social media platforms. For the uninitiated, the team explains how to use the Internet on a smartphone and how to get social media apps on these phones. In fact, Ramdev could charge ad fee from mobile companies for his yoga camps often propagate how mobile Internet packs are so cheap and easy to get. There is an easy comparison. 'It's as easy as to use the TV remote,' says a team member on the mike.

The thrust on social media doubled following a widespread report—again circulated on social media—which claimed that Ramdev had suffered a heart attack. Photographs of him being carried on a stretcher surfaced on Facebook. Ramdev came up with a strong rebuttal: '*Jisko bukhaar hi kabhi nahi hota, usko heart attack kaise hoga* (How can a person who never gets sick get a heart attack?)'

But social media has not always been kind to the yoga guru. When I did his profile for *India Today* magazine, the cover—shot exlclusively by Bandeep Singh, my colleague and one of India's best photographers (his designation of that of a Group Photo Editor speaks little of his achievements)—went viral and instantly he became a butt of jokes. After a day-long trip with Ramdev, who drove us around his multiple factories and offices in Haridwar in his Scorpio, Bandeep photographed him at his ashram. As usual, Bandeep wanted an unusual cover photograph and we requsted him to bend to his front and pop out his head between his legs. We did not know if there was any yogic posture like this but Ramdev did it effortlessly. And he did it multiple times, holding the position for minutes together. In an article in *DailyO*, Bandeep explained why he clicked the Baba the way he did. I take the liberty to quote from it here:

When India Today decided to do a cover story on Baba Ramdev, my biggest challenge was to create an image which people have not seen. An image that would arrest attention and draw you to pick the issue up to flip inside. In the barrage of celebrity images that leap at you in the public domain, Baba Ramdev's face is as ubiquitous as Narendra Modi's. How do you photograph a news celebrity who is now also staring at you from every hoarding of Patanjali—which is fast becoming a remarkable business success story to come out of India in this decade. The picture had to somehow reflect this. Whew.

On our way back I hear my colleague Kaushik Deka and Baba Ramdev discuss his business mantra.

I was already thinking yoga postures and I heard 'ulta'. That was the shirshasana. Babaji's well-known statement about MNCs flashed in my mind. 'I will make all of them (MNC executives) do shirshasana,' he said somewhere. I was now feverish with excitement.

A Baba taking on the multinationals and in the wake creating a mega brand with hundreds of products of daily use and a profit line that is going into astral space. It disrupts many stereotypes. It's actually turning corporate logic upside down and in the process spirituality upside down—a shirshasana! I had my concept.

A personal note: On 9 November 2016, a day after Prime Minister Narendra Modi's historic declaration banning currencies of ₹500 and ₹1,000 to weed out black money and fake currencies and stop terror funding, I had a brief telephonic conversation with Ramdev. He asked me to tweet that he initially propagated the idea of banning high value notes in 2010. I obliged him.

ॐ

Yoga: A Cure for All

Ramdev has regularly courted controversy with his claims to cure fatal diseases like cancer and AIDS through yoga and pranayama (a breathing exercise).

In an hour-long video titled 'Yog cancer ke liye', which is available on YouTube and on his website, Ramdev claims he has been able to cure several types of cancer, including brain tumours, with a concoction of wheat grass juice, tulsi and leaves. 'You can consume 10 to 50 ml of this juice. Start on this if there is no improvement with chemotherapy or radiation. Consume as much as you can digest. There is no side effect of this juice. With this treatment, we have seen that blood cancer can be cured. I am telling you this because we have data and have also published results of our research,' Ramdev tells his followers in the video. Along with wheat grass, he also recommends a daily regimen of pranayama for cancer treatment.

In another 4-minute video titled 'IIT Student Cured from Cancer by Yoga', the yoga guru showcases how he has cured a student of IIT Kharagpur, who had been suffering from pancreatic cancer. Here is the full text of the conversation between Ramdev and the student which is available on the Internet along with the video.[23]

> Ramdev: He has studied in IIT... IIT KHARAKPUR... Then he got cancer. During the last year of his studies.
>
> Student: First, the cancer got developed in pancreas, then it spread to kidneys...
>
> Ramdev: First, the cancer got developed in pancreas, then it spread to kidneys...multiple places
>
> Student: Cancer tumour turned 1.5 kgs...haemoglobin was 6.2...
>
> Ramdev: I did not also know that...tumour was 1.5 kgs.
>
> Student: Then, I started doing pranayama for the full day...
>
> Ramdev: I am surprised!!!! Pranayama for the full day!!!!! but, how did u develop the will to do pranayama?? Highly educated boys generally tend to be casual. This is his commitment. Full day pranayama!!!
>
> Student: I used to see you on TV since 2005. Thought of doing it, but later when I developed cancer, I searched on the internet, is there anything else apart

---

[23]http://bharatswabhimansamachar.in/iit-student-cured-from-cancer-by-yoga-baba-ramdevpatanjali-yogpeeth/

from pranayama, chemotherapy will only cure it by 2 to 10 per cent, so...

Ramdev: 2 to 10 per cent assurance for chemo, he read it on the net that pranayama can help. So, full day pranayama? (asking the student)

Student: After lunch, 4 hours of anulom vilom, 4 hours of kapalbharti...

Ramdev (Laughing): I also never thought of that...He is always doing duty nowadays. He leaves pranayama to do seva, but I scolded him. Leave all the work. First, do pranayama, then only you should do seva. Do not leave pranayama. Come on, sit with me and do it now.

Ramdev: All the cancer patients get up. See this boy. He is like your child. All the old ladies and gents. He is an example for all of us. He cured his cancer, dangerous of 1.5 kg tumour with 4 hrs of rigorous pranayama only. So, you should also take a leaf out of him.

Ramdev (asking the student): Did your parents allow you? How many of brothers and sisters are you?

Student: Only one. Parents are liberal. One sister got married.

Ramdev: I have called him personally to show it to everybody about this. He is a manmauji. Going to guru, his parents did not stop him.

Though, Ramdev has declined ever making any statement

saying that he can cure HIV/AIDS, the homepage of www.yogapranayama.com, which sells his products reads: 'On India TV & couple of other TV Channels, on December 22 and 23, 2006, Swami Ramdev Ji said that Yoga Pranayama & the Ayurvedic & Herbal Medicines suggested by him can control & cure AIDS. He added that the CD4 cell count of the people affected by AIDS, which had fallen to 50, 100, 150 have gone up to 400, 500, and even 600, which is quite normal. He added that even the people with CD4 cell count of 5 to 10 have benefitted. CD4 cells (T4 count, T-helper cells) are a class of immune cells that gradually get depleted in HIV infection. India TV also showed a lady, declaring openly, in one of his Yoga Science camps to have been cured of AIDS. This lady had come to know that she had AIDS after she lost her husband due to AIDS.'

The September 2006 issue of the monthly *Yog Sandesh* says on page 55: 'Yoga Guru Swami Ramdev while addressing the people said that Yoga & Pranayama have been successful in curing 200 cancer patients and he is ready to give evidence. The ancient science is also beneficial in case of AIDS and experiments are being carried out in that area. He would make formal announcement once the tests are completed.'

A release by NACO on 22 December 2006 reads: 'A section of the media has reported the claim made by Baba Ramdev that yoga can cure AIDS. He is also reported to have claimed that AIDS cannot be prevented by using condoms. While yoga and regular exercise certainly help people including those who are HIV positive to be healthier, it would be far-fetched to claim that a cure for AIDS will be found through yoga in the next couple of years. The reported statement may mislead the masses and undo the immense efforts that countless social activists, volunteers and organizations have rendered over the years to check the spread of the epidemic by promoting safe behavioural practices. Further, the reported suggestion by Baba Ramdev to do away with sex education among youngsters will be a retrograde step. The demand of the time is to open up discussions on the issues of sex and sexuality and break the silence surrounding HIV/AIDS. Information and knowledge is the only way of saving the lives of our youths.'

Union Minister of State for AYUSH, Shripad Naik has said that Ramdev's claim regarding the cure of HIV/AIDS will be clinically checked by the government. 'We will get details from him. We will have to get it clinically cleared,' Naik told reporters, in response to a question whether his ministry will examine the claims of the yoga guru that he can cure cancer and AIDS.

When dengue became rampant in Delhi in 2015, claiming nearly two dozen lives, Ramdev said that Patanjali Yogpeeth had done several procedures and came out with scientific preventive measures against the disease. He also suggested a homemade remedy to prevent the disease. 'A 50 ml mixed juice of Giloy, aloe vera, papaya leaf and pomegranates given daily can prevent dengue,' he said.

It's not cancer, AIDS and dengue only. The yoga guru claims to have cure for the 'disease' of protests and strikes in industrial units. Speaking at the Happening Haryana global investor summit, which was held two weeks after the state was brought to a standstill by violent protests by Jats for reservations, Ramdev offered to deliver motivational speeches to employees in big industries and hold yoga classes to put an end to strikes and hartals. 'Industries pay huge fees for getting people to deliver motivation speech. I will do it for free for your employees. Obviously, it may not be possible for me to come to every unit. But I can address people in big units. *Mein hartaal aadi ki bimaari ko bhi theek kar doonga,*' he said.

ॐ

Baba as Brand Ambassador

While most consumer firms spend around 10–15 per cent of revenues in advertising and publicity (A&P), Patanjali has done it without any meaningful A&P investment so far, says a Credit Lyonnais Securities Asia (CLSA) report. 'We spend very less on advertising and I'm a free brand ambassador,' says Ramdev. Even after Patanjali's dedicated distribution network of outlets, the Patanjali products are present in less than 0.2 million outlets compared to the 2–7 million for peers. No wonder, Patanjali has hired two top advertising agencies McCann and Mudra to prepare the business for the next phase of growth. In FY16, the company kicked off a television and print advertising campaign, forged alliances with big-box retailers like the Future group and entered the e-commerce channel. The impact is visible. From dance reality shows to newspaper front pages, Patajali now is omnipresent.

According to industry sources, the group spent nearly ₹400 crores in advertising, but if Baba Ramdev has to be believed, it's less than ₹60 crore. 'We do hard bargaining,' says Balkrishna. According to Anuja Chauhan, creative consultant for advertising agency JWT India and a writer, 'Patanjali is riding on Ramdev's huge fan following. The company got two things right—one, the whole India-ayurveda connection and, second, the MNC style of advertising.'

In 2016, Patanjali Ayurved inserted as many as 1.14 million advertisements across television channels, as per data from viewership measurement agency BARC India. Patanjali advertisements were displayed on TV channels for 7,221 hours across 161 channels. That translates into an average of 19 hours 43 minutes of advertising time every day. Patanjali is now among the top 10 advertisers in the country.

Interestingly, 84 per cent of total advertisements that Patanjali aired in 2016 played on news channels, and nearly 99 per cent on Hindi news channels. That's one way of reining in costs since this genre is cheaper than GECs (general entertainment channels) but it also means missing out on a core audience. The rest of the FMCG pack relies on entertainment channels to sell their products because news channels have a relatively small share of the viewership pie—English news at 0.03 per cent, Hindi news at 3 per cent and regional news at 3.5 per cent, as per KPMG-FICCI.

However, targeting news channels is a strategy which media planners say has helped Baba create brand pull amongst traders and viewers alike. According to Anand Chakravarthy, managing partner at Maxus India, Patanjali, by advertising heavily on news channels, which is viewed by many traders, has been creating trade confidence.

Distribution is the backbone for FMCG and through news channels, Patanjali is reaching out to small traders. In a way, it's persuading these traders to stock up its products, rather than opening their own stores at every nook and corner.

From a wrestling league to bhajan shows on television to talk shows on FM radio, Patanjali Ayurved Ltd is on a sponsoring blitz, supporting almost everything that appeals to young people, has a desi link, or both. Patanjali, which had co-presenting rights for the Kabaddi World Cup in 2016, is now sponsoring season two of Pro Wrestling League, besides television serials such as *P.O.W.—Bandi Yuddh Ke* on Star Plus and *Waaris* on &TV, and dance show *Super Dancer* on Sony. Baba Ramdev wrestled with Olympic silver medalist Andriy Stadnik as part of promotions for Pro Wrestling League. Though nobody knows if it was staged or real, Ramdev easily defeated Stadnik.

The sponsorship drive aims to target young people in urban areas—a segment where Patanjali has not really seen the kind of success it has seen in other segments. However, the swadeshi philosophy remains intact, as the company will be associated only with Indian sports and events that build on Indian culture. Patanjali has officially declared that it will not sponsor cricket, as it's not an Indian game.

According to experts, Ramdev's participation ensures higher viewership given his following and that helps Patanjali bag sponsorship deals at lower costs. Patanjali is estimated to be spending up to a fourth of its advertising and promotional spends on sponsorships. The episode of popular comedy show *Comedy Nights with Kapil* when Baba Ramdev appeared earned more TRPs than the *Big Boss* episode where Salman Khan and Shah Rukh Khan appeared together.

While media buyers and industry experts estimate that the company spent ₹400 crore last year and will spend ₹600 crore this year, Patanjali's spokesperson claims that the entire advertising and marketing spend is just about 10 per cent of what Hindustan Unilever Ltd (HUL) spends in a year. In 2016, HUL spent ₹4,595.18 crore on advertising and promotions, a little over 14 per cent of its net sales of ₹32,482.72 crore. Vermillion Communication and Combined Advertising handle Patanjali's media buying.

However, Patanjali has also been mired in controversies following accusations of misleading advertisements of its products. On 15 December 2016 a court in Uttarakhand slapped Patanjali Ayurved with a fine of ₹11 lakh for 'misbranding and putting up misleading advertisements.' Patanjali Ayurved was found guilty of misbranding as the products being shown by the company as produced at its own units were in fact manufactured somewhere else, the court said. A case had been filed in the court against the company in 2012 by the District Food Safety Department after samples of mustard oil, salt, pineapple jam, besan and honey produced by Patanjali had failed quality tests at Rudrapur laboratory.

The products were found to be in violation of sections 52–53 of food security norms and section 23.1 (5) of food safety and standard (packaging and labelling) regulation.

This was not the first time Patanjali has got into trouble. According to industry rivals, Patanjali has often made exaggerated claims in advertisements while it takes digs at other companies for the same. The ASCI pulled up Patanjali Ayurved for 33 advertisements between April 2015 and July 2016 appearing in various media such as TV, print and product packaging, and in various sectors such as food and beverages, personal care and healthcare.

In several advertisements, Ramdev and Balkrishna themselves appear to be urging consumers to either shun brands of 'foreign' companies or not to get carried away by claims of products, which allegedly contain harmful chemicals. They offer Patanjali products as the safe and natural alternative to these products. However, these appeals have not gone down well with authorities such as the Food Safety & Standards Authority of India and the Advertising Standard's Council of India (ASCI). ASCI is an independent regulatory body that monitors advertisements to check for false claims. These agencies have accused Patanjali of grossly exaggerating its products' benefits while showing other brands in poor light. In response, Ramdev questioned the authority of ASCI calling it 'unconstitutional'. 'They cannot pass any judgement against the non-members. There are several judgements against them. Its order is not binding on any non-member.' 'They do not have any expert on Ayurveda and life science. How can they decide these things arbitrarily? They do not have any laboratory. What is the authenticity of their decision?' said Ramdev.

On 14 August 2016 Ramdev had filed a defamation suit and notice of motion against ASCI (seeking interim relief against the latter) for getting a series of notices on their advertisements from the regulatory body in recent months. Patanjali's rival Dabur had earlier complained to the advertising watchdog about Patanjali's advertisement claims on honey, which it thinks contains 'misleading' and 'unsubtantiated' claims on purity, according to reports. Patanjali has, through its advertisements, laid claim to its honey as being 'Purity ki Double Guarantee'.

This was not taken too well by Dabur, and it filed a case against the firm's advertising claims to the ASCI. Acting upon the complaint, the ASCI has directed Patanjali to either 'withdraw or modify its advertisement'. Patanjali maintained that it had conducted more than 100 tests on its honey on the basis of parameters established by BIS and FSSAI. Ramdev's company then claimed that ASCI had no experts on board to verify Dabur's complaints against its honey in the reports.

Here are some instances when Patanjali was censured by ASCI for presenting 'misleading' facts in their advertisements.

Divya Swasari Pravahi: The advertisement claims, 'Thousands of banned medicines are being sold in the market. The harmful results of these bad chemicals are surfacing now. Thousands of pharmaceutical companies are paying crores of rupees as a fine for this act. Besides this, health of people is getting affected by these chemicals.' According to ASCI, this claim is factually incorrect and not substantiated with authentic supporting data. Such a claim denigrates competition and puts the entire allopathic cough and cold medicine category in bad light. Also, the claim saying that Divya Pharmacy Ayurvedic medicines have no side effect and 100 per cent results has not been substantiated and is misleading, says ASCI. The advertisement also claims that lakhs and crores of people have used this product for over twenty years.

Divya Mukta Vati & Divya Madhunashini Vati: Some of the statements on the advertisement were— 'Conducting trials on over 1 crore people.' 'It gives strength to pancreas and naturally controls diabetes.' 'It also controls the most dangerous side effects of diabetes like neuropathy, nephropathy and retinopathy.' ASCI says these claims were not substantiated and are grossly exaggerated.

Patanjali Dant Kanti: Again, ASCI says that the advertisement's claims—'the trusted brand of crores of countrymen', 'herbal toothpaste', 'long duration protection and full profit of this product goes to educational charity'—are not substantiated and are misleading by ambiguity and exaggeration.

Patanjali Kesh Kanti Shikakai Hair Cleanser: The ASCI objects to the advertisement's claim that the product reduces hair fall, greying and itchy scalp.

Patanjali Kesh Kanti Reetha Hair Cleanser: The ASCI says the advertisement's claim that the product strengthens roots is not substantiated and misleading.

Patanjali Kesh Kanti Natural Hair Cleanser: The advertisement's claim of the product alleviating hair fall, hair breakage and dryness was flagged by ASCI.

Patanjali Kachi Ghani Mustard Oil: The advertisement makes a sweeping statement that a majority of the products in the market are adulterated with addition of cheap palm oil. According to ASCI, there is no authentic evidence to support this statement and the advertisement is misleading by exaggeration. The advertisement also unfairly denigrates other oil products by calling them cheap adulterants.

Patanjali Jeera Biscuit: The advertisement's claim that the biscuit contains 100 per cent atta, has no cholesterol and is low on 'sodium salt' has not been substantiated. It's also misleading by ambiguity, as the advertiser does not provide any quantitative declaration of the various ingredients used in the manufacturing of the product. The advertisement claims the benefits of jeera (cumin), showcasing it as the single ingredient, but its presence in the product was not substantiated to signify its quantity in the product. Also, presentation of certain claims on the package—rich in iron, increases haemoglobin and helps in acidity and other stomach-related problems—is misleading by implication as these may be the benefits of cumin but the text implies that the biscuit will provide those benefits.

Wearing His Opinion on His Sleeve

Since his debut on Sanskar channel in 2001, Ramdev has understood the power of media in capturing and formulating the public opinion. He is very well versed with the way media functions and knows how to make it work in his favour. With his eyes constantly fixed on the public mood, Ramdev knows how to feed the TRP-hungry TV channels with the spiciest quotes. And that's the reason he has an opinion on everything under the sun. And that's why TV journalists love him. Here is a brief compilation of Ramdev's response to some issues of national relevance, which made news.

BHARAT MATA KI JAI

This is one episode Ramdev would have liked to erase from public memory. As a swadeshi brand warrior, Ramdev wears his patriotism on his sleeve, or to be apt, on his langot. In fact, he has installed a statue of Bharat Mata right at the gate of the acharyakulam located inside the campus of Patanjali Yogpeeth. When RSS sought to hijack the entire discourse on Bharat Mata by making chanting of 'Bharat Mata ki Jai' a yardstick of patriotism, Ramdev certainly did not want to be left behind. Speaking at a Sadbhavna rally organized by the RSS in Rohtak—attended by Himachal Pradesh Governor Acharya Devvrat, among others—Ramdev said: '*Koi aadmi topi pehan kar ke khada ho jaata hai, bolta Bharat Mata ki Jai nahi bolunga, chahe meri gardan kaat do. Arey is desh mein kanoon hai, nahi toh teri ek ki kya, hum toh lakhon ki gardan kaat sakte hain. Hum is desh ke kanoon aur samvidhan ka samman karte hain, nahi toh koi Bharat Mata ka apmaan kare, ek nahi, hum hazaron lakhon ke sheesh kalam karne ka samarth rakhte hain.* (Some person wears a cap and stands up. He says I will not say Bharat Mata ki Jai even if you decapitate me. This country has a law, otherwise let alone one, we can behead lakhs. We respect this country's law and Constitution, otherwise if anybody disrespects Bharat Mata, we have the capability of beheading not one but thousands and lakhs.)'

Ramdev's outburst came against the backdrop of AIMIM Chief Asaduddin Owaisi's remarks that he will not chant 'Bharat Mata ki Jai' even if a knife is put to his throat. A bitter reminder, however, came from Uttar Pradesh Minister Azam Khan who called Ramdev just a vaidya and asked him to confine to his own business. 'How a person who had fled from Ramlila Ground (in Delhi) by putting on a woman's dress can talk of beheading those raising dissenting voices,' said Khan referring to the police crackdown on Ramdev's rally in Ramlila Maidan in June 2011.

Of course, Ramdev expressed regret later about making that statement. In a private conversation with me, he admitted that he had got carried away and as a yogi he should not have made such comments, but what he would never accept in public or private is that he got the limelight he was seeking. With one sweeping statement, he established his 'patent' over the slogan of Bharat Mata ki Jai. There were people before him giving soundbites on Bharat Mata, there will be people after him making noise about Bharat Mata, but every voice will be drowned in Ramdev's threat, which he says he never meant.

The guru, however, may face legal trouble as a case has been registered by Hyderabad police under section 295A (deliberate and malicious acts intended to outrage religious feelings) of the IPC, but that could be a small price to pay.

DRUGS AND PUNJAB

In May 2015, Ramdev claimed that 80 per cent of youths in Punjab had fallen prey to drug menace. 'Whenever I travel abroad, people keep telling me to do something about this and save Punjab,' Ramdev said in a press conference.

A year later, in 2016, Ramdev made a volte-face. 'A campaign is underway to malign the image of Punjab that it is a state where a majority of youths are into drugs, but this is not the ground reality,' he said while delivering a special lecture at a yoga session in Panjab University. He said the youth in Punjab was full of energy and into constructive work, which were not being highlighted.

Interestingly, no journalist reminded him of his comment of 2015, but there were questions about the Congress party's proposed protest against drug menace and deteriorating law and order situation in the state the next day at Jalandhar where Congress Vice-president Rahul Gandhi was supposed to be present. Ramdev lost no time in taking a dig at Rahul for whom the yoga guru seems to have special aversion. 'One should first ask him whether he took drugs in his life ever,' Ramdev quipped.

MEDICINE 'ENSURING' SON

On 1 May 2015, Janata Dal (United) Rajya Sabha MP K.C. Tyagi waived in the upper house a packet of 'Putrajeevak Beej', which he claimed to have bought from Divya Pharmacy on 14 April. Tyagi claimed that this fertility medicine promised the delivery of a male child, which is illegal, and therefore it must be banned and Ramdev must be brought to book. In a deliberate attempt to embarrass the Modi government, he said: 'Ramdev is the brand ambassador of BJP-ruled Haryana. This is against the Prime Minister's campaign of "Beti Bachao, Beti Padhao".'

Union Health Minister J.P. Nadda was quick to react: 'The government will look into it and proper action will be taken. The government is very serious about the sex-ratio. The PM was personally monitoring the "Beti Bachao, Beti Padhao" campaign,' said Nadda.

Union Consumer Affairs, Food and Public Distribution

Minister Ram Vilas Paswan said: 'It is a gender issue. If you are asking for only a male child, it is illegal.'

However, amid political uproar, what everyone missed out on is that the medicine—which is easily available in all Patanjali stores for ₹35 per packet and also through online portals—never promised a male child and the confusion was the result of its misleading name. The botanical name of the controversial medicine 'Putrajeevak Beej' is 'Putranjiva roxburghii'. Its name has misled many politicians and even doctors, who claimed that 'Putrajeevak' translates as 'son's life', thereby meaning the consumption of this medicine would guarantee a son. 'MPs who have no clue about Ayurveda should be ashamed and should apologize to the nation. The medicine (pack) does not say anywhere that it helps in producing a son,' Ramdev said in a press conference in New Delhi.

Acharya Balkrishna was sober with his explanation: 'Due to its name, people might consider it to be a medicine which helps in conceiving a male child. This herbal medicine is a result of Ayurvedic experiment, which helps a childless woman to conceive. Putrajeevak Beej is most effective if taken with Shivlingi seeds and this natural remedy is in use since thousands of years ago in India.'

However, despite his close relationship with Ramdev, Madhya Pradesh's Chief Minister banned the medicine in his state. The State government has asked Patanjali Yogpeeth to first change the name of the medicine to obtain permission to sell the product in Madhya Pradesh. Ramdev, however, remained adamant and said that he would not change the name, though he agreed to add a disclaimer to the medicine highlighting that it won't help couples have a male child in particular.

THE 'HOMOPHOBIC GURU'

At an *India Today* Conclave in 2008, its then editor Prabhu Chawla asked Ramdev about his views on homosexuality. Making a gesture through his hand showing how he eats his food, Ramdev said: 'I take my food straight to my mouth, like most of us do.' Then he made another gesture, first taking his hand behind his head and then bending it to reach his mouth. 'If some people want to have his food like this, what can I say?'

But Ramdev has a lot to say about homosexuality. He was ecstatic when the Supreme Court gave its verdict holding consensual sex between adults of the same gender an offence. 'The Supreme Court has respected the sentiments of the various religious communities of India. Today they are talking of homosexuality, tomorrow they will talk of having sex with animals.' Section 377 of Indian Penal Code terms homosexuality as unnatural and carries a maximum punishment of ten years in jail.

For Ramdev, homosexuality is a disease and yoga can certainly cure it. 'Homosexuality is not genetic. If our parents were homosexuals, then we would not have been born. So it's unnatural,' he has said. What's more, he has even questioned the intellectual prowess of homosexuals by openly claiming that gay community has very little contribution to the field of science and economics.

Even the RSS could not soften Ramdev's stand on homosexuals. At the 2016 *India Today* Conclave, RSS Joint General Secretary Dattatreya Hosabale said that homosexuality was not a crime though he later tried to make amends by saying that it was a 'socially immoral act'. 'No need to punish [homosexuality], but to be treated as a psychological case,' Hosabale had tweeted.

Ramdev was quick to reject Hosabale's view saying that homosexuality was immoral and unnatural. 'RSS should rethink its stand on homosexuality,' Ramdev told a news agency.

HIS BLACK MONEY CONTROVERSY

The crusader against black money himself got embroiled in an embarrassing controversy when he was caught on camera murmuring to the BJP candidate from Alwar Lok Sabha constituency, Mahent Chandnath: 'Are you a fool asking and talking about money when cameras and mic are on?'

Moments before a press conference, in front of a bunch of cameras and microphones, Chandnath told Ramdev that '*Paise le aane mein badi dikat ho rahi hai* (Facing problems bringing money here)' and Baba Ramdev wanted to shut him up saying, '*Yahan baat karna bandh karo, bhole ho kya?* (Stop talking here, are you a novice?)'

PADMA AWARDS

Two days before the awards were to be presented on 26 January 2015, Ramdev had claimed that he had written to

Home Minister Rajnath Singh declining the award as he came to know that he was being considered for it. On 6 November 2015, he spurred fresh controversy by claiming that he was denied a Nobel Prize because of his complexion.

While the Nobel claim resulted in social media jokes, an RTI response to activist Subhash Agrawal later revealed that Ramdev was never considered for the honours. To a query seeking to know the names of persons who were shortlisted for the civilian honours but turned it down, the Home Ministry said Salim Khan, former diplomat K.S. Bajpai and spiritual gurus Sri Sri Ravi Shankar, late Mohammed Burhanuddin and Mata Amritanandamayi had refused to accept the Padma awards.

ON AWARD WAPSI

In the run up to the 2015 Bihar Assembly polls and following the lynching of Akhlaq in Dadri, Uttar Pradesh, the country saw several luminaries returning government awards in protest against growing atmosphere of intolerance since the Narendra Modi-led NDA government came to power. Ramdev had his own take on the issue:

> Many incompetent and undeserving people seem to have got awards and cheap politics is going on in the name of award return. Country's image is being tarnished on international platform.
>
> A majority of those returning the awards have got the laurels with backing of Congress and the Left parties. This is nothing but attempts to please those political

parties and their leaders. Only returning the laurels on namesake will not do. They must return the money they earned with the award.

From whatever little I have understood of Swami Ramdev through my interactions with him and all that I have read about him, I have understood one thing definitely—there will be many more controversies surrounding him in future. For one thing, he still has not mastered diplomacy and has little chance of ever being politically correct. To many people, he may have political ambition—in fact he almost launched a political party—but he can never be a politician. His views are strong and straight—you may agree with him or you may laugh at him. But it's very unlikely that he will stay away from public glare. Because he is one guru who prefers the din of public life than the silence of the Himalayas.

❧

Acknowledgments

I have always wanted to write a book, rather hundreds of books, but could never bring myself to write even the first sentence. It's perhaps the most difficult task in the world—to write the introductory line of a book. Writing has always been a comical exercise for me. I got into 'serious writing' only after I joined *India Today* magazine, which gave me the confidence that I can write on anything on earth—from the Northeast to national politics, from price mechanism of petrol to vagaries of monsoon. And the person responsible for making me such a versatile 'expert' is our Executive Editor S. Sahaya Ranjit. One fine day, he had asked me to interview Baba Ramdev for our High and Mighty issue. For this book to have happened, the first credit goes to him.

The second biggest contribution came from India Today Group Editorial Director Raj Chengappa, who chose me to do the profile on Ramdev when the editorial board decided to do a cover story on the yoga guru. But it's not only the cover story on Ramdev. In the last two years,

Chengappa has given me the opportunity to do the most exciting stories of my career and I can never thank him enough for it. His presence and logical approach to work explains the importance of a mentor in the growth of any professional. Saying just thanks to him actually demeans his contribution.

I probably could not have had an easy access to Ramdev if I did not have the patronage of India Today Deputy Editor Uday Mahurkar. One of the most generous human beings I have ever met in my life, his kind words about me immensely helped in the Yoga Guru opening up to me.

Another just as kind individual is S. Prasannarajan, Editor of the *Open* magazine. Officially, he is my former boss, but I can still reach out to him for any professional advice. He did not take a second to grant me permission when I sought to use a paragraph from an article published in *Open* for my book.

Last but not the least, I must mention a very important person involved in this effort. Several publishing groups approached me to write a book on Ramdev after the *India Today* cover story had been published. I perhaps did do a decent job, but the story would not have drawn such attention if India Today Group Photo Editor Bandeep Singh had not shot the cover. His magic behind the lenses made the story go viral and the rest is history. A big thank you to Bandeep.

I must also not forget India Today Editor (Special Projects) Kaveree Bamzai, who has played a key role in my growth as a journalist over a decade. She had been pushing me to write a book for quite some time. I know she is a difficult boss to please, but I have always tried hard.

Technically, I must express my gratitude to my parents, wife, sister, relatives and friends for their support, love and affection. But I will not do any such thing. Simply because what else are they supposed to do? It's my birthright and their noble duty. I'm happy and proud to have them in my life and they should reciprocate the feeling.

Hope you all enjoy my book.